The Path of Revival

Restoring Our Nation – One *Church* at a Time

By Mark R. Barnard

9157

Published by ChurchSmart Resources

We are an evangelical Christian publisher committed to producing excellent products at affordable prices to help church leaders accomplish effective ministry in the areas of Church planting, Church growth, Church renewal and Leadership development.

For a free catalog of our resources call 1-800-253-4276.
Visit us at: www.ChurchSmart.com

Cover design by: Julie Becker

ISBN-10: 1-889638-86-2
ISBN-13: 978-1-889638-86-7

SDG

The Path of Revival

If my people who are called by my name

Revival begins when God's people see
They are in need of recovery

Shall humble themselves

The Church must face the painful truth
Spiritual blindness may be at the root

And pray

Prayer is the Church's desperate plea
She cries for removal of complacency

And seek my face

God reveals His opinion
He displays the Church's weakened condition

And turn from their wicked ways

God's people must yield and break
All God shows them they must forsake

Then will I hear from heaven and forgive their sin and heal their land.

Healing, recovery, revival come
The Church freshly blessed by God's son

2 Chronicles 7:14

Table of Contents

Acknowledgements

Four years ago I read a book titled, *Healing the Heart of Your Church*, by Dr. Kenneth Quick. It was one book among several that I received from my friend Tom Bowden, church planting director for the South Atlantic District of the Christian and Missionary Alliance. As I sorted through the box of books Tom sent, something in my spirit led me to focus on Dr. Quick's book. As I read its pages I was strongly impressed that its content was specifically designed for the church where I served as interim pastor. Several months later the book's principles of corporate healing demonstrated their curative effect. I am convinced that church would not be here today had their leadership not recognized the relevance of the book's message. Since then many churches have benefited from *Healing the Heart of Your Church*.

Often, however, these churches were in dire straits before they willingly considered their need of healing and spiritual revitalization. The purpose of *The Path of Revival* is to take the principles of corporate healing and present them in a way that broadens the scope of their application. Hopefully the ideas found within will appeal to and prove helpful for churches before they need to head for the emergency room.

In an effort to facilitate spiritual health in churches across this nation and beyond, Blessing Point Ministries was formed. Blessing Point works to heal and revive the hearts of local churches and revitalize the Body of Christ. This ministry could not function without the encouragement, prayers, and leadership of people like Nancy Griffin, Robert Palmer, Tom Bowden, Tom Duddles and Dr. Ken Quick. (Those familiar with Dr. Quick's work will recognize my indebtedness to his teaching, particularly in the latter chapters of this volume. I owe him a debt of gratitude for his editorial work on the initial draft of this book as well.) These dear folks serve on the board of Blessing Point and are passionate about restoring the radiance of Christ's Bride. Neither could I personally function in this capacity were it not for the encouragement, wisdom and faith of my own bride – Jeannie.

Blessing Point believes the Lord longs for each local church to be blessed in its work and witness. We believe local church leaders are God's people in a tough job. We value them! We believe that when a local church wrestles with a lack of meaningful ministry there are often divinely established preconditions that must be met before God will bless. Our prayer is that you and your church would enjoy a fresh, compelling sense of God's blessing on your ministry. We pray that through the fresh sense of blessing you receive many might be brought into the Kingdom through the ministry of your local church.

For the advance of His kingdom,

Rev. Mark Barnard – President
Blessing Point Ministries - Strengthening Churches to Soar
www.blessingpoint.org

Chapter One

The Church, Churches and the Nation

"What America needs more than anything else right now is to know she cannot exist without the worldview that helped bring her into existence."

- Ravi Zacharias

Driving on a back road in rural Georgia, a song on the radio caught my ear. Sung by Loretta Lynn and Conway Twitty, its heartfelt cry summarizes the burden of this book:

> "God bless America again
> You see all the trouble that she's in
> Wash her pretty face, dry her eyes and then
> God bless America again
>
> God I sure do wish you'd bless America again
> You know like you did way back when it all began . . ." [1]

Those simple lyrics suggest that somewhere along the line America lost God's blessing. The song implies something changed since the time when it "all began." It assumes that a nation can enjoy divine favor and that it can be lost as well.

---

[1] Boyce Hawkins and Bobby Bare, *God Bless America Again*, <http://www.metrolyrics.com/god-bless-ameri ca-again-lyrics-conway-twitty.html>.

Does a sense of national blessing erode? How does the loss of such blessing manifest itself? If such blessing has been lost, can it be regained, and if so, how? Who can mediate such a re-blessing?

These questions tumble to mind as we reflect on America's current condition. Economic stresses, natural disasters, wars, and declining moral standards challenge us from all sides. Can we honestly say we enjoy the blessing we once did? Today's politicians often end their speeches with "And may God bless America!" How timely it would be for such a speech to end with; "And may God bless America – *Again!*"

The Premise

America's growing problems are not rooted in a lackluster economic model, questionable political policies, the breakdown in the family, or the explosion of evil in our midst. These symptoms reflect a deeper problem. Neither the deeper problem nor its cure resides in secular society. William Wilberforce, known for his efforts to free England from the slave trade in the late 18th century, writes in his book *Real Christianity* as if he were among us today. He says, "The problems we face as a society should be viewed as *spiritual problems* rather than merely political issues. This is a perspective that does not even appear to be considered by the media. What can we expect from the kinds of solutions they offer? Certainly they would only produce transient progress, not fundamental change"[2] (Italics mine.).

Addressing fundamental change in society means casting off mistaken assumptions as to the nature of our nation's woes. We have come to believe that our problems are of a moral, political or economic nature. (The Enemy loves for us to think that way.) When in reality, our problems are fundamentally *spiritual*. Spiritual problems will not be solved by any government program or by any media-promoted agenda.

If our societal problems are primarily spiritual, where do we go for help? To find solutions we must go to the source of the problem. This brings us to my main premise: *Spiritual problems suggest something is wrong not merely with the nation but in the heart of the Church.*

In his book, *The Living Church*, John Stott says, ". . . if society becomes corrupt there is no sense in blaming society for its corruption. That is what happens when

---

[2] William Wilberforce, *Real Christianity* (Ventura, CA: Regal Books, 2006) 177.

human evil is unchecked and unrestrained. The question to ask is: Where is the Church?"[3] It is not as if the Church is absent from the scene. Signs of her presence are found everywhere, from fish symbols to Christian radio stations to steeples pointing skyward in towns across the nation. In spite of her presence across the landscape, the Church suffers from a steep decline of influence. Stott lays out the current religious situation with clarity: "Most countries today are increasingly pluralistic in both race and religion. That is to say Christianity, Islam, secularism, materialism, ancient religions and modern cults are all competing for the soul of our country. Which is going to win?"[4]

> "In spite of her presence across the landscape, the Church suffers from a steep decline of influence."

How has the American Church lost its competitive edge and what impact does this have on the current state of the nation? I propose that a lack of blessing on the Church makes it weak and unattractive to our culture. The deficit of Divine blessing we sense on our nation stems from the lack of His blessing on the Christian Church. Wilberforce describes one of the symptoms of a less-than-blessed Church when he writes, "Yet what we see today in Christendom is a practice of Christian Faith that often produces no greater morality than that practiced by those who categorically deny the essentials of the Christian faith." [5]

We who love the Lord may not agree that Wilberforce's assessment is true of our time. But a glaring disparity of opinion exists between believers and nonbelievers on the relevance and attractiveness of Christianity. Blame it on the postmodern mindset, on the belief that all religions are created equal, or perhaps on the many stains found on the Bride of Christ. Whichever explanation we choose, Christians must acknowledge that if the Bride of Christ glistened with renewed radiance, nothing could stop the ensuing positive cultural transformation. Nothing could stop the re-blessing of America.

What has brought us to our current state? How has the faith responsible for the establishment of the colonies and whose spiritual passion birthed this nation become so weak and sickly? How is it that secularism's influence has been on the rise and the Church's in distinct decline? What's wrong in the heart of the Church?

---

[3] John Stott, *The Living Church* (Downers Grove, IL: IVP Books, 2007) 134.
[4] Stott 128.
[5] Wilberforce 65.

Anesthesia of the Soul

Anesthesia of the soul is a coping mechanism. It enables us to deal, or perhaps not deal, with the plethora of difficulties we face. Daily reports of violence and disaster assault our emotional and spiritual sensitivity. The sheer quantity of disturbing news we encounter bombards our sanity. We just cannot handle the volume of distressing news to which we are exposed. We choose numbness to protect ourselves from the constant drain on our emotions.

The medical world documents this phenomenon. Researcher Robert Jay Lifton, studying the survivors of Hiroshima and other disasters, calls it "psychic numbing." It works like this, "In a situation in which our emotional feelings are overwhelmingly painful or unpleasant, we have the capacity to anesthetize ourselves. It is a simple sort of thing. The sight of a single bloody, mangled body horrifies us. But if we see such bodies all around us everyday, day after day, the horrible becomes normal and we lose our sense of horror. We simply tune it out. Our capacity for horror becomes blunted. We no longer truly *see* the blood or smell the stench or feel its agony. Unconsciously we have become anesthetized."[6]

Many of us in the Church have lost our sense of horror. The horrible has become normal and we must find some way to cope. How many abortions does it take before we don't want to think about them anymore? How many action alerts from the American Family Association does it take before we don't want to open their emails? How many minutes in front of the evening news can we endure before we switch to a sports channel, or the History or the Food channel?

Tuning out painful realities produces numbness and numbness produces dumbness. This is not the dumbness of ignorance as if to suggest we are ill-informed because we can't bear to watch the evening news. Rather we are dumb in the sense that we have lost our voice. John Dawson writes in, *Healing America's Wounds*, "This is a land of refuge, outreach and example; however, the American Church has lost it's voice, and this in part is because we do not know what to say . . . If we do not speak out a godly dream for this nation, the ship of state will lose its rudder and drift with the wind."[7] Those words were written fourteen years ago. Fourteen years of drifting have passed. Where has our numbness gotten us?

Two biblical passages address the problem of spiritual anesthesia. The first, Matthew 24:12, predicts a cultural shift in emotional disposition during the days prior to Christ's return. "*And because lawlessness is increased, most people's*

---

[6] Scott Peck, *People of the Lie* (New York: Touchstone, 1983) 221.
[7] John Dawson, *Healing America's Wounds* (Ventura, CA: Regal Books, 1994) 129.

4

love will grow cold." This affirms the research done by Lifton. Overexposure to wickedness leaves us "cold" to the normal feelings of compassion that love motivates. It also anesthetizes us to the sense of justice that love demands.

The second passage shows that some events can so disturb people that they unify the godly ones in the face of wickedness. Judges 19-20 tells a story that starts out sordid enough. A Levite took for himself a concubine. What was this religious man doing with a *concubine* anyway? As the story unfolds, the concubine prostitutes herself and then flees to her father's house in fear. The Levite chases her down and reconciles with the wayward woman. The couple travels to Gibeah. There the men of the town seize the concubine and, as verse 25 sadly reports, *"the men . . . raped her and abused her all night until morning then let her go at the approach of dawn."* She crawled home and died on the doorstep.

The offense was so heinous and the method used by the Levite to awaken a sense of righteousness so extreme that it broke through the spiritual anesthesia of God's people. Judges 19:29-30 reveals, *"When he entered his house he took a knife and laid hold of his concubine and cut her in twelve pieces, limb by limb and sent her throughout the territory of Israel. And it came about that all who saw it said, 'Nothing like this has ever happened or been seen from the day when the sons of Israel came up from the land of Egypt to this day. Consider it, take counsel and speak up!'"*

Do you find the Levite's actions shocking? God's people of the Levite's era found them so. What of a similar nature would shock us out of our numbness? What would it take to arouse the sense of horror we have lost?

Prosperity Problem

Though we evangelicals may find ourselves at odds with the "prosperity gospel," we have far more difficulty addressing the thorny problem prosperity may cause *us*. We enjoy a high standard of living in this country. In spite of recent setbacks, we enjoy the highest quality of life the world has ever known. How long can Christians enjoy the general prosperity of a nation and yet maintain their distinctive calling and influence? Prosperity facilitates our cooperation with the world-system. How long can we function in that environment without selling our souls?

What happens if our prosperity is suddenly threatened? The writer of Hebrews reminded his audience: *"But remember the former days, when after being enlightened, you endured a great conflict of sufferings, partly by being made a* *public spectacle through reproaches and tribulations, and partly by becoming sharers with those who were so treated. For you showed sympathy to the prisoners, and **accepted joyfully the seizure of your property**, knowing that you have for yourselves a better possession and an abiding one"* (Hebrews 10:32-34).

For the original recipients of the letter to the Hebrews, the seizure of their property was a price they were willing to pay. What if the government forced Christians in this country off their property through an unjust application of the law of eminent domain? Would we accept that seizure *joyfully?*

Prosperity creates difficulties when the believer becomes comfortable with a high standard of living. (Ironically, God may be addressing this problem through the economic problems we now face.) Wilberforce alluded to the same dilemma in his day, "In times like we are living in, ideas of radical obedience and self denial fade into the background. Even faithful Christians become soft and more tolerant of the moral decline of the world around them."[8] If we fail to recognize the sedative effect prosperity has on us, there is little hope for anything but continued silence in the face of evil. If we overvalue our rights and possessions, fear of losing them makes it difficult to speak up in the face of unrighteousness. We have been bought with a price, the Bible tells us, but perhaps we've sold our influence for pennies on the dollar.

Spiritual Lethargy

Emerson once wrote, "Man is as lazy as he dares to be." Is it possible that we are just too lazy to pay a price, sacrifice and seek the Lord afresh? The early believers faced a similar struggle. Augustine admonished the believers of his day, whose non-intervention within secular society betrayed their self-interest. He writes, "For often we wickedly blind ourselves to the occasions of teaching and admonishing them (*unbelievers*), sometimes even of reprimanding and chiding them, either because we shrink from the labor or are ashamed to offend them, or because we fear to lose good friendships, lest this should stand in the way of our advancement, or injure us in some worldly matter, which either our covetous disposition desires to obtain, or our weakness shrinks from losing."[9] (Italics mine).

Self-interest keeps us from substantive intervention in the way things are. In other words, spiritual laziness does not occur by accident. Comfort with the status

---

[8] Wilberforce 143
[9] Saint Augustine, *The City of God* (New York, NY: Random House, 1993) 11.

6

quo (and the fear of destabilizing it) is the source of our laziness. Confronting evil means *discomfort*. When laziness and apathy infect the Church, we must confront ourselves before we can regain our influence in the world or confront evil. Confronting *ourselves* is the starting place for revival.

Sin in the Camp – Wounds in the Heart of the Church

Regardless of their denominational status, many local churches have histories marked by painful episodes of conflict and hurt. The wounds inflicted have never been addressed. The effects of unhealed wounds or unrepentant hearts in the life of a church leave it limping along with a limited sense of blessing. Such a state requires us to take a hard look at a church's spiritual history. In spite of the *need* to do so, local churches demonstrate a tremendous reluctance to examine themselves.

But if churches ignore problems in their corporate histories, how can they be prepared for revival should it come? Will it not pass them by? Will God bless an entity with unresolved sin in its history or unhealed corporate wounds? No and no again. Local churches that hope for revival without a season of serious corporate reflection fool only themselves. Church splits, a lack of church discipline, abusive pastors, heavy handed church boards, shameful incidents, faithless decisions, financial and moral improprieties, and sinfully reactive behavior do not go overlooked by the Lord. These hinder revival and require corporate repentance.

Richard Owen Roberts writes in his book titled, *Repentance*, "It is generally understood that every individual sins and needs to repent. Many however, have never considered the problem of corporate sin and the mandatory nature of corporate repentance. Yet it is a fact that just as every individual sins, so does every corporate entity. One of the most damaging mistakes of the present day is the prevailing tendency to overlook the problem of corporate sin and the need of corporate repentance. When corporate sin occurs but no corporate repentance follows, the offending entity falls under the judgment of God. That judgment is normally remedial, and it remains in place until either true repentance is exercised or God sends a final judgment of death and destruction."[10]

Local churches must seek the Lord's face to hear what He is saying to them. If your church, or denomination for that matter, wants to see revival, it must put itself in a blessable state by taking a hard look at its history and rectifying anything

---

[10] Richard Owen Roberts, *Repentance* (Wheaton, IL: Crossway Books, 2002) 57.

that hinders God's blessing. The next Great Awakening may await a multitude of tarnished, unhealthy churches regaining a fresh sense of God's blessing and power for ministry. It's a tantalizing possibility.

But even if such a revival proved elusive, it is incumbent on every local church to respond to the Lord about any corporate wounding and sin. Why should we struggle with the Enemy's foot on the neck of our ministry because of such unresolved issues? Unresolved corporate sin, wounds or pain limits our ministries as if they were chained to an invisible cement truck filled with hardened concrete. Laboring under such conditions leaves pastors and lay leaders looking for the nearest exit. We begin to doubt everything—our call, God's promises and purpose—everything when we serve in the context of corporate dysfunction for long periods of time.

> "We begin to doubt everything – our call, God's promises and purpose – everything when we serve in the context of corporate dysfunction for long periods of time."

A discouraged church elder once asked me if there were such things as "Ichabod churches." You will recall Ichabod was the name given to a child whose mother died giving birth in 1 Samuel 4. She went into labor upon hearing that her husband and brother-in-law were killed in battle, and that the Ark of the Covenant had been captured. "Ichabod" was the last word on her lips. It means "no glory," as in "God's glory has departed from Israel." The capture of the Ark meant God's glory dwelling with Israel was gone.

So what then do we make of the frustrated elder's question about "Ichabod churches?" His question assumes that things can go so wrong in the local church that we begin to wonder if God's glory has departed! The term "Ichabod church," suggests that some congregations function Sunday after Sunday without a clear sense of God's blessing. Christ's letters to the seven churches in Revelation tell us He walks among the candlesticks. So we know His presence is evident even in churches with great need of repentance, but how many churches operate without any sense of His blessing?

Personal vs. Corporate Revival

Finding an answer to the problems in the heart of the Church may seem daunting. But restoring the full radiance of Christ's Bride comes through personal and corporate revival. We need both. Most current revival teaching revolves around the spiritual life of the individual. But the biblical teaching on the re-blessing of God's people is anchored in the corporate setting. The Lord spoke after a Solemn Assembly at the dedication of Solomon's temple in 2 Chronicles 7:14 when He said, "*If my people who are called by my name will humble themselves, and pray, and seek my face, and turn from their wicked ways, then will I hear from heaven and forgive their sin and heal their land.*"

A great assembly of people saw God's glory fill that temple. The guest list was expansive. 2 Chronicles 5:2-3 records, "*Then Solomon assembled to Jerusalem the elders of Israel and all the heads of the tribes, the leaders of the fathers' households of the sons of Israel, to bring up the ark of the covenant of the Lord. . . And all the men of Israel assembled themselves to the king at the feast.*" The priests and the Levitical singers were there, as well as the temple musicians. And most importantly the glory of the Lord showed up for the occasion.

The verse we use so often in the context of personal revival was made in response to a corporate assembly. God made His specific promise of revival in a night time appearance to *King Solomon* as the representative head of the *nation*. The Lord used 2 Chronicles 7:14 to describe His future policy toward the nation of Israel, the unique *group* of people set apart to Him.

We then see where 2 Chronicles 7:14 sets out the conditions of God's blessing on His people as a *whole*. He called His people to humble themselves corporately, to pray corporately and seek His face corporately. They were called to turn from their "wicked ways" corporately. Corporate revival receives far less emphasis in teaching and preaching, but it is the primary focus of every Old Testament revival.

In the New Testament, Jesus' letters to the seven churches of Asia focus on the same things. Congregations were held accountable for their corporate condition. Jesus called the majority of those churches to repent as *corporate* entities. Would not corporate repentance anticipate corporate revival?

In corporate revival we're not talking about tweaking a church's program of ministry, but rather addressing spiritual roadblocks to God's blessing on that ministry. *Just as sin hindered God's blessing on the nation of Israel, sin and wounds in the body of Christ hinder God's blessing on local churches.* Though a multitude of helps exist for churches seeking to implement the latest ministry practices, few address this core issue. How have we overlooked it for so long?

The majority of teaching focuses on personal revival because it reflects the individualistic perspective of our culture. In the early preaching during the formative years of our nation, this individualistic approach was not always the focus. Early American preachers had a clear sense of corporate accountability before God. That is not to say we do not need revival to occur on an individual level. There is little benefit to getting our corporate houses in order if we have not thoroughly dealt with our individual hearts. We need both corporate and personal revival.

In the pages that follow we will explore revival in general as well as it's personal and corporate implications. Our hope is to recapture the biblical mandate to address corporate failings that limit the scope of God's blessing, particularly on the local church and, by extension, on the Church at large.

I believe that ignoring corporate revival and its requirements has led to the demise of churches and denominations. In previous revivals, God bypassed certain churches and even whole denominations. What if those old organizational structures addressed the corporate wounds and sin in their history and were ready when the new wave of awakening arrived?

Instead, their lack of responsiveness often necessitated the birth of new movements through which God could work as He willed. One needs only remember Jesus' warning to the *church* of Ephesus, to grasp the urgency and relevancy of our topic. *"Remember therefore from where you have fallen, and repent and do the deeds you did at first; or else I am coming to you and will remove your lampstand out of its place – unless you repent"* (Rev. 2:5). In other words: repent corporately or it's lights out! This is the powerful role corporate repentance and revival play – the re-blessing of His people as an entity, particularly as a local church.

Summary

David Olson surveys the contemporary spiritual landscape in his book, *The American Church in Crisis* and writes, "A chill wind is blowing in America, affecting the future of Christianity. Most of the basic indicators point downward . . . will the future become a dark night of winter for the Church or will spring break forth and create new life?"[11] The answer to that question rests within the heart of the Church at large and more specifically within the heart of each local church across this country. Can God bring us to new health and vibrancy? Can we shake off the spiritual anesthesia? Can we loosen the desensitizing grip

---

[11] David T. Olson, *The American Church in Crisis* (Grand Rapids, MI: Zondervan, 2008) 182.

prosperity has on our hearts? Can we overcome the spirit of lethargy? Can we be healed from the wounds in the history of our churches that leave us limping along? The answers may seem uncertain, but some things are not.

Here is my point: The re-blessing of America rests squarely with the re-blessing of the Church. The re-blessing of the Church rests with the re-blessing of a multitude of local churches. Jesus calls us to repentance and revival as local communities of believers. Revelation 3:19 says, *"Those whom I love, I reprove and discipline, be zealous therefore, and repent."* It is up to us. We must look at Church history and soberly recall He has bypassed and even removed ministries that proved unresponsive to His discipline in the past.

I pray both our nation and Church reach the *blessing point* together. May we see a new work of God in our time. May it start with individual congregations and their leaders having the courage to hear from and respond to the Lord of their church. May our radiance as His Bride be renewed. May it result in a new era of positive cultural transformation. And may God bless America – *Again*!

Chapter Two

If my people ...

"Ordinary Christianity is not enough, more is demanded. Are we not beginning to feel that nothing can deal with this situation but a manifestation of true life and living, holy living as it is under God? And if not why not?"

- Martin Lloyd Jones

"The power of God seemed to descend upon the whole assembly 'like a rushing mighty wind.' And with astonishing energy bore down on all before it. I stood amazed at the influence that seized the audience almost universally and could compare it to nothing more aptly than the irresistible force of a mighty torrent . . . Almost all persons of all ages were bowed down with concern together and scarce one was able to withstand the shock of this surpassing operation."[12] David Brainerd penned these words in 1745, describing a move of God among a tribe of American Indians. His account stirs us to a righteous jealousy to see the same spiritual energy released in our day. Could God's "astonishing energy" and "irresistible force of a mighty torrent" find its way into the Twenty-First century?

In the previous chapter we established the defining text directing us toward the re-blessing of God's people: 2 Chronicles 7:14. It is the passage we turn to when the topic turns to a new work of God in our midst. *"If my people who are called*

---

[12] Stephen F, Olford, *Lord Open the Heavens!* (Wheaton, IL: Harold Shaw Publications. 1969) 60.

by my name will humble themselves and pray and seek my face and turn from their wicked ways, then will I hear from heaven and will forgive their sin and heal their land" (NIV). What is the blessing point to which we aspire in revival? It is where we receive the benefits contained in this power-packed Scripture verse.

When the spiritual energy of its promise gets released among us, we are freshly assured that "the gates hell will not prevail" against the church (Matthew 16:18). We find ourselves emboldened for the gospel. The fruit of our witness flows freely as the presence and power of God get released among us. The transformation of culture begins as God's people regain their sense of blessing, functioning as salt and light in a dark and decaying world. The need to experience these benefits frequently draws us back to the promise God made to Israel many years ago.

This verse occupies center stage in much of the preaching we hear on the subject. Preachers have leaned on it to exhort people to experience a fresh, new, and powerful work of God. They often sought to capture the essence of revival in their own words. Dr. Stephen Olford put it this way, "Revival is that strange and sovereign work of God in which He visits His own people, restoring, reanimating and releasing them into the fullness of His blessing."[13] A. W. Tozer describes the power of the Holy Spirit released in times of revival when he writes, "I mean that effective energy which God has, both in biblical and in post-biblical times, released into the Church and into the circumstances surrounding her, which make her fruitful in labor and invincible before her foes."[14]

Vance Havner says, "What we call revival is simply a return to normal New Testament Christianity. Most of us are so subnormal that if we ever became normal we would be considered abnormal!"[15] Did you follow that? Revival leaves us appearing abnormal in comparison with our culture or with a less potent strain of Christianity. John White, in his book *When the Spirit Comes with Power*, puts revival in context: "Most significant movements start by being a little wild, settle down to respectable middle age, then rejoicing in their respectability, relax into creeping death."[16] He adds "Revival is war."[17] Staving off creeping death is a battle! We fight for the very life of Christ's Bride!

Charles Finney writing early in the 19th century said, "Revival is the renewal of the first love of Christians, resulting in the conversion of sinners to God. It

---

[13] Olford 15.
[14] A.W. Tozer, *Paths to Power*, (Harrisburg, PA: Christian Publications) 11.
[15] Vance Havner, *Messages on Revival*, (Grand Rapids, MI: Baker Book House, 1958) 15.
[16] John White, *When the Spirit comes with Power* (Downers Grove, IL: InterVarsity Press, 1988) 178.
[17] White 35.

presupposes that the church is backslidden and revival means conviction of sin and searching of hearts among God's people. Revival is nothing less than a new beginning of obedience to God, a breaking of heart and getting down in the dust before Him with deep humility and forsaking of sin. A revival breaks the power of the world and of sin over Christians." [18]   And Dr. Martin Lloyd Jones writes of revival, "It is a kind of sign that God gives . . . in order to confirm His work in the Church, and to establish His people . . . it overflows in mighty blessing to those who are without."[19]

These definitions capture our imagination. We desire to see such a revival in our day. The Scriptures have much to teach us about the viability of such a hope. We want to review this material in a manner that helps us prepare for a new work of God in our midst. First and foremost, we must know what revival looks like. A review of the Old and New Testaments reveals four concepts related to revival.

Four Biblical Concepts of Revival

Recovered Health and Healing

Revival is closely identified with recovered health and healing. The end of 2 Chronicles 7:14 brings this out, ". . . *then will I hear from heaven and forgive their sin and **heal their land**.*" This verse to which we turn in regard to revival does not even mention the word "revival"! Rather, upon meeting the conditions of the verse, God promised the nation of Israel *healing*. When the Bible speaks of healing in this context, what should we understand? The word "heal" here is the Hebrew word, *raphah*. Its root is used to describe mending, as in stitching pieces of cloth or fabric back together. It includes the idea of repairing or making thoroughly whole,[20] as when a physician cures, not simply the symptoms, but the root cause of an illness. In this context, the word speaks of the restoring of Israelite land previously cursed. God chose to inflict non-productivity of the land to get His people to pay attention. Agriculture was the economy in Solomon's day. When God disciplined His people, He hit them where it hurt – in the wallet. But if they met His conditions, the land would be healed and again bring forth fruit.

This concept of healing shows up in other contexts, such as in Jeremiah. "'*But I*

---

[18] Havner 15.

[19] Martin Lloyd Jones, *Revival* (Westchester, IL: Crossway Books, 1987) 15.

[20] James Strong, *A Concise Dictionary of the Words in the Hebrew Bible* as published within *The New Strong's Exhaustive Concordance of the Bible* (Nashville: Thomas Nelson Publishers, 1984) 110.

*will **restore you to health and heal your wounds**', declares the LORD, 'because you are called an outcast, Zion for whom no one cares'"* (Jeremiah 30:17). Jeremiah addressed the Israelites in the early stages of the Babylonian captivity. He predicted the restoration or revival of the nation some seventy years later. One can only imagine the damage that needed healing as a result of being forced out of their homeland and being made refugees in a foreign land. The national psyche would need lots of repair work. But the primary focus here reveals that God promised a day when the nation would be healed in the sense of reestablished. It would not languish forever. The Lord planned to restore them to health and treat their painful wounds. Jeremiah 33:6 elaborates on the resurgence of the nation in the days to come. *"Behold, I will bring to it **health** and **healing** and I will **heal them**."*

The prophet Hosea used the same image. He combined revival and healing in the same declaration. *"Come, let us return to the Lord. For He has torn us, but He will **heal** us; He has wounded us, but He will bandage us. He will **revive** us after two days; He will raise us up on the third day"* (Hosea 6:1-2). The word "heal" here is the same one used in 2 Chronicles 7:14 and Jeremiah 30:17. When Hosea describes God as having "torn us," "heal" makes sense given its meaning to mend as in the stitching of a torn garment. But the idea of healing as in the restoring of health is not far behind, for healing is also used relative to being *"wounded."* The word *"revive,"* closely tied to the idea of healing, brings to mind the idea of experiencing new life, the very thing one would expect to feel when restored from severe wounds.

There is a secondary and relevant application of the phrase *"and heal their land."* The land was the real estate that made up the Israelite nation. Divine discipline caused the land to decline agriculturally. Productivity, prosperity and the general well-being of society diminished as a result. They faced challenges in economic decline, famine, and drought. This was God's message to them that there was a problem in their relationship with Him. But just restoring the land to productivity may be too narrow given the references to healing found in Jeremiah and Hosea. Healing Israel's relationship with God was the primary focus, not simply restoration from famine or drought. The curse on the land was symptomatic of the spiritual health of the people. As such, the concept of "healing the land" may be applied more broadly to the healing of the society that occupied the land.

Restored spiritual health among God's people therefore brings societal benefits. Revival transforms culture and heals the land in this broader sense. It restores order and moral backbone, and produces social reform and conversions to God's kingdom. The effects of revival can heal the entire culture. The influences of evil become retarded. Israel regains their national distinctives as God's people. They would enjoy the benefits of that healing as spiritual health permeated society. Healing of the land has broader social and cultural implications than just the restoration of agricultural productivity.

The broader sense of healing is what most people intuitively think of when they read 2 Chronicles 7:14. Revival brings benefits to the nation among whom the people of God reside. As God's people restore their relationship with God, the changes in their hearts affect the social agenda. Wilberforce wrote about the connection between a new move of God and social improvement: "If, by God's grace, a new wave of true spirituality were to break forth and gain ground, there is no way of predicting the way public morals and the political welfare of the nation would benefit. The encroachment of toxic decay would be forced to cease. The blessings of God would once again be released in our land."[21]

> "Are we willing to consider the possibility that evangelical churches are suffering spiritual ill health?"

Isn't that the vision we covet for our nation? And yet we cannot escape one particularly potent observation. If revival is closely associated with healing and restored spiritual health, what does that suggest about the *pre-revival* state of God's people – the Church? Are we willing to consider the possibility that evangelical churches are suffering spiritual ill health? Do we really believe that? What are we doing with our symptoms? Do we tolerate these symptoms hoping they will go away on their own? Or are we willing to go to the One who holds the promise of healing us totally?

In the passages we reviewed, each referred to God's people as an entity, *not* as individuals. Each addressed the *nation* of Israel. Individual believers are touched by revival but the healing promised always applied to the corporate entity known as Israel. If we take any application from this, it is that God's work to which we aspire is described consistently as *corporate* revival and more specifically corporate *healing*.

These principles of corporate healing and revival are applicable to us corporately today. They work in the Church at large and particularly in the local church. In fact they *only* work in the Church at large to the extent they work in local churches. God's people, whatever the size or location of their ministry, can regain spiritual

---

[21] Wilberforce 158.

health through the principles of corporate revival.

What about your church? Is it in need of corporate healing? Have wounds been inflicted on your local body whose lingering effects still limit you, maybe decades after they occurred? We may overlook, minimize or ignore them, but the Lord of the Church knows and these issues are still alive before Him. If your church has languished because of unaddressed traumas, the healing promise of revival should appeal to you. Attending to our corporate wounds prepares us for a literal reviving of our corporate energies.

Renewed Blessing

The Bible connects revival and a renewal of God's blessing. The Prophet Haggai wrote, "*Is the seed still in the barn? Even including the vine, the fig tree, the pomegranate and the olive tree, it has not borne fruit.* **Yet from this day on I will bless you.**" (Haggai 2:19) This minor prophet makes a major point. He describes the moment of blessing, the "blessing point" to which we aspire.

Haggai's two chapter account describes a people who grew content while the Jerusalem temple lay in ruins. After the initial wave of Jews returned from Babylon, sixteen years after they laid the foundation, the temple sat desolate. What were God's people up to during this period of time? What preoccupied their minds and distracted them from finishing the temple? Here's what the Lord said about them, "*Thus says the LORD of Hosts, 'This people says, "The time has not come, even the time for the house of the LORD to be rebuilt."' Then the word of the LORD came by Haggai the prophet saying, 'Is it time for you yourselves to dwell in your paneled houses while this house lies desolate?' Now therefore, thus says the LORD of hosts, 'Consider your ways!'*" (Haggai 1:2-5) Here was God's sticking point with His people. They put off rebuilding the temple but found plenty of time to upgrade their homes. They grew insensitive to God's priorities as reflected in the luxury of their "paneled houses" as compared to the destitute condition of the temple.

It is likely that the remnant having returned to Jerusalem not only ignored the condition of the temple but after a while did not even see the condition of the temple. They grew blind to the physical condition of the structure. They got used to a run down temple facility, and became preoccupied with their own priorities. They found satisfaction in upgrading their decor while God's house lay in ruins. This disparity became the focus of Haggai's message. He leveled a one-two punch in his double admonition to "*Consider your ways*" in 1:5 and again in 1:7.

Haggai also helped the occupants of Jerusalem understand why they had not enjoyed the success for which they hoped. Note the dynamic of diminishing returns the prophet describes: *"You have sown much, but harvest little; you eat, but there is not enough to be satisfied; you drink, but there is not enough to become drunk; you put on clothing, but no one is warm enough; and he who earns, earns wages to put into a purse with holes"* (Haggai 1:6). It is as if God's people had just enough to exist but never enough to prosper. Their situation deteriorated with resources chewed up by unexpected needs.

The Israelite economy was not the problem but the symptom. The problem they did not even know they had was hidden from their eyes. God hoped the pain of their lean harvests and financial drain would cause them to seek His face. Haggai revealed the close connection between their root problem and the dire straits in which they found themselves when he wrote, *"'You look for much, but behold, it comes to little; when you bring it home, I blow it away. Why?' declares the LORD of hosts, 'Because of My house which lies desolate, while each of you runs to his own house. Therefore, because of you the sky has withheld its dew, and the earth has withheld its produce. And I called for a drought on the land, on the mountains, on the grain, on the new wine, on the oil, on what the ground produces, on men, on cattle, and on all the labor of your hands'"* (Haggai 1:9-11). The last phrase is especially poignant, " ***on all the labor of your hands***." Their efforts to advance their well-being would be fruitless until they addressed the issue that stood between them and God.

However, the story of Haggai had a positive outcome. It encourages us for the struggles we face. The Israelites reached the blessing point after they finally reached the turning point of "considering their ways." Thank goodness they did! *"So the Lord stirred up the spirit of Zerrubbabel the son of Shealtiel, governor of Judah, and the spirit of Joshua the son of Jehozadak, the high priest, and the spirit of all the remnant of the people; and they came and worked on the house of the LORD of hosts, their God"* (Haggai 1:14). As they began to rebuild the temple, God encouraged them over and over. He assured them that He was with them (1:13; 2:4). He told them not to be afraid and that His Spirit was abiding with them (2:5). He assured them that He would fill the house they were rebuilding with His glory (2:7). He let them know that He had all the resources they needed to accomplish His will (2:8). He promised them His peace (2:9). He gave them a vision of the future and though their work seemed like nothing in their eyes, the latter glory of the temple would exceed the former! (2:9)

No more would they suffer under divinely-imposed discipline. God rescinded the law of diminishing returns previously placed on them. The prophet Haggai reiterates God's former policy toward them then goes on to state that they will enter a new era of blessing. "*'I smote you and every work of your hands with blasting wind, mildew, and hail; yet you did not come back to me,' declares the Lord . . . 'Is the seed still in the barn? Even including the vine, the fig tree, the pomegranate, and the olive tree, it has not borne fruit.* **Yet from this day on I will bless you.***'"* (2:17, 19).

There was a policy change in heaven! Formerly they struggled under the corrective influences of almighty God, but they listened to the prophet and demonstrated evidence of authentic repentance. The response from heaven was immediate. God's disposition toward them radically changed. The revival recorded in Haggai's day demonstrates that, when we respond to the Lord's discipline as a people, we can expect to enter a new era of blessing. Fruit takes the place of frustration and blessing replaces divine discipline.[22]

Fresh Outpouring of the Holy Spirit

Of all the biblical concepts related to revival, a fresh outpouring of the Holy Spirit represents the most common when we anticipate a dramatic new work of God. It must be noted that the Great Awakenings in America all bore the signature of the Holy Spirit's outpouring, even as at Pentecost when the Holy Spirit first made His presence known in the early church. "*When the day of Pentecost had come, they were all together in one place. And suddenly there came from heaven a noise like a violent rushing wind, and it filled the whole house where they were sitting. And there appeared to them tongues as of fire distributing themselves, and they rested on each one of them and they were* **all filled with the Holy Spirit**" (Acts 2:1-4).

The subsequent boldness displayed by Peter and the rest of the early believers resulted in a massive influx of people into God's kingdom. The Holy Spirit came a second time in Acts 4:31 to reanimate God's people. "*And when they had prayed, the place where they had gathered together was shaken, and* **they were all filled with the Holy Spirit** *and began to speak the word of God with boldness.*"

We know that reviving does not come from the exertion of our own energy. We need to be reenergized by a source of power other than our own. The Holy Spirit lives in every believer and we each yield to Him to varying degrees in our daily lives. It is His goal to increase the territory of our heart under God's control. God constantly works out the progressive aspect of our sanctification. But in revival, He orchestrates an event where He reanimates us, reorients us, and revitalizes us.

---

[22] See also Deuteronomy 28:1-14 for signs of God's blessing on a people.

It is dramatic, undeniable and sometimes even controversial.

The personal and corporate aspects of revival converge in the outpouring of the Holy Spirit. Many individual lives were touched by God's Spirit in Acts 2 and 4, but it was also a *corporate expression* of God's blessing. In revival an *attractive* quality infuses a church. The whole body receives the blessing of God *not just its individual parts*.

One may ask, "What does a recovery of God's blessing look like in a local church?" It looks just like Acts 2:42-47:

> "They were continually devoting themselves to the apostles' teaching and to fellowship, to the breaking of bread and to prayer. Everyone kept feeling a sense of awe; and many wonders and signs were taking place through the apostles. And all those who had believed were together and had all things in common; and they began selling their property and possessions and were sharing them with all, as anyone might have need. Day by day continuing with one mind in the temple, and breaking bread from house to house, they were taking their meals together with gladness and sincerity of heart, praising God and having favor with all the people. And the Lord was adding to their number day by day those who were being saved."

We get another glimpse of what God's corporate blessing looks like in Acts 4:32-35:

> "And the congregation of those who believed were of one heart and soul; and not one of them claimed that anything belonging to him was his own, but all things were common property to them. And with great power the apostles were giving testimony to the resurrection of the Lord Jesus, and abundant grace was upon them all. For there was not a needy person among them, for all who were owners of land or houses would sell them and bring the proceeds of the sales and lay them at the apostles' feet, and they would be distributed to each as any had need."

Revival affects the spiritual climate of a church long after the initial outpouring. As we begin again to relate to each other in loving and God-honoring ways, the corporate health of the body improves. We start to see the above evidences in our local assembly. A relational climate-change begins to occur. New spiritual health and blessing permeate our congregation. Olford writes, "Someone has described revival as a 'person or community saturated with the presence of God.' This is an accurate description for when God breaks into a life or community, nothing else matters save the person of Jesus, the glory of Jesus, the name of Jesus. Revival is not some emotion or worked up excitement. It is rather an invasion from heaven which brings to man a conscious awareness of God."[23] The radiance of Christ's Bride starts to shine as the Holy Spirit awakens a renewed awareness of Christ in our midst.

Revival Starts with God's People

In 2 Chronicles 7:14 it is clear that revival starts with God's people. Just as the Gospel is the power of God "*to the Jew first and also to the Greek*" (Romans 1:16), so revival is the power of God to the Church first and also to the world. This is the divine order of the blessing released in revival. It starts with God's people: "*If **my** people who are called by **my** name…*" Revival starts with us, not with the lost.[24]

The implications of revival starting with God's people are both encouraging and daunting. Let's talk about the encouraging part first. "*If my people who are called by my name*" demonstrates God's commitment to His people in their pre-revival state. He considers them His people even when they are in great need of revival! He claimed them as His people, not once, but *twice* in the same breath. He invites their return to Him even in the midst of their ignorant rebellion.

When the Bible describes the benefits of revival, two are specifically mentioned. The latter we have already examined says, "*and will heal their land.*" But the former is just as crucial: "*I will forgive their sin.*" Contained in that simple promise is the restoration of the sin-damaged relationship between God and His people. God knew that the nation of Israel would go down the wrong road. He foresaw the problem and 2 Chronicles 7:14 was designed for their plight.

For God to anticipate the rebellion, sin and cultural compromise of His people and to still lay out the path of revival stands as the greatest of romantic stories. God had no misconceptions about human nature, even among those who claimed His name. Revival starts with God's people for the simple reason that God loves us enough to restore us when we return to Him. How beautiful is that? He endures our faithlessness, idolatry and fickle devotion, calling us back to Himself through circumstances designed to awaken the remembrance of His love. The simple requirements He lays out in 2 Chronicles 7:14 are magnanimous. The conditions make the prospect of reconciliation attractive to the wayward party.

---

[23] Olford 60.
[24] John Dawson, *Healing America's Wounds* (Ventura, CA: Regal Books, 1994) 92.

God does everything He can to encourage the people He claims as His own to return to Him.

Now let's consider the daunting part. God's people must start the process! From a historical perspective, the likelihood of Israel doing so was often in question. Their willingness to humble themselves, turn to God in prayer, seek His face and turn from their wicked ways proved skittish at best. Revival, when it came, did so only after painful periods of national corporate discipline through famine, drought or war. Revival starts with God's people but they don't always come willingly. Divine discipline often precedes spiritual sanity. Until God's people come to their senses and begin to respond to God, the remaining promises of 2 Chronicles 7:14 can never be fulfilled.

If they meet the conditions outlined, forgiveness and restoration follow. The forgiveness He promised assured the Israelites (as it does us) that if they return to the Lord, He returns to them. As we come to understand how we also have deviated from Him and repent, He will return again to bless the Bride He loves. 1 Peter 4:17 tells us that *"judgment begins with the household of God."* That's just where revival starts too – with God's people.

Again, this means the collective body feels the impact of revival. This is far removed from evangelistic services held in church and labeled "revival meetings." That is not true revival. Revival starts with God's people. As God's people revive, then the lost can be reached. The attractiveness and radiance of a blessed and healthier congregation draws others through its doors. God trusts such a people with those He wants to draw to Himself because He has cleansed its corporate heart and restored its spiritual health. We know how God uses individuals whose hearts are clean before Him. The same is true of local churches.

Now what about *your* people and *your* church? Can you imagine greater spiritual health and blessing entering your fellowship? Can you imagine the Holy Spirit working powerfully in and through your congregation? Revival need not be something we read about or for which we wish. A new work of God begins when God's people—and that includes *your* people—start responding to Him.

Putting it All Together

Combining these four biblical concepts related to revival, we come closer to an accurate biblical definition. This gives us a starting place for concern and prayer. It sets our expectations and gives us an idea of what we hope to see realized in revival. Revival includes the concepts of recovered spiritual health, renewed blessing, a fresh outpouring of the Holy Spirit, and corporate responsiveness to God on the part of God's people. When we combine those four biblical concepts we can state it as the following definition: ***Revival is a fresh encounter with God's Spirit among God's people resulting in a recovery of God's blessing***.

Revival restores our relationship with God and each other so that it more closely resembles the book of Acts. It radically restructures hearts, priorities, relationships, outlook, boldness, and love for the Lord. The recovery of God's blessing is a collective blessing. It impacts believers as a *body*, as a corporate whole. The recovery of God's blessing also affects us qualitatively. The fresh awareness of God alters what we and the world have come to think of as Christianity. It enlivens our hearts, and the Bride of Christ regains her beauty and radiance God destined for her. In the light of this renewed radiance, a church enjoys an attractive quality that draws people to Christ. As such churches multiply, gaining new strength and health, God builds up the Church at large. Then it is only a matter of time until the change in the heart of the Church influences the decay and darkness of the nation.

Chapter Three

If my people, who are called by my name ...

"Let us think of the need of souls, of all the sins among God's people, of the lack of power in so much of the preaching, and begin to cry, 'Wilt thou not revive us again; that thy people may rejoice in thee?'"

- Andrew Murray

On November 5th 1740, English evangelist George Whitefield preached at the fledgling Presbyterian church in Basking Ridge, New Jersey. Of the experience, "Whitefield wrote afterwards, 'I had not discoursed long, but in every part of the congregation somebody or other began to cry out, and almost all were melted to tears . . . One cried out, 'He is come! He is come!' and could scarce sustain the discovery that Jesus made of himself to his soul. Others were so earnest for a like favor, that their eager cries compelled me to stop. Most of the people spent the remainder of the night in prayer and praise. Oh, it was a night much to be remembered!"[25]

The night Whitefield described demonstrates how the Spirit of God works mightily among God's people in times of fresh blessing. Revival, as we have noted, begins with God's people. And, to make doubly clear this starting point, God proclaimed, *"If my people, who are called by my name."* We see in the opening phrase of 2 Chronicles 7:14 where the conditions of revival rest. The

---

[25] Dorothy L. McFadden, Mildred D. Van Dyke and Eileen L. Johnston, *The Presbyterian Church* Basking Ridge, NJ A History www.brpc.org-publications-BRPCHistory1717-1989.pdf 6.

Lord could have made His point by leaving the opening phrase, *"If my people."* But there is explicit emphasis with the addition of, *"who are called by my name."* He does not want it to escape our notice that the blessing we need starts with initiative on our part.

To take such initiative, we need to understand the biblical significance of revival. In the previous chapter we explored some of the biblical concepts of revival found in the Old and New Testaments. We combined those concepts and arrived at a biblical definition: ***"A fresh encounter with God's Spirit among God's people resulting in a recovery of God's blessing.""*** This definition focuses on the goal of revival. 2 Chronicles 7:14 outlines the principles to get us there. But the Bible further illumines the path of revival and it is to those passages we now turn our attention.

Biblical Settings of Revival

The Old and New Testaments show that revival takes place in two settings. Revival occurs in both the personal and corporate arenas. We want to balance the scales upon which these two aspects are weighed. Most Scripture is weighted on the side of corporate revival, but the weight of contemporary teaching is on the side of personal revival. These two emphases must be recalibrated. We've put so much emphasis on personal revival that corporate revival gets forgotten. We largely divorce personal spiritual health from corporate spiritual health. We seek revival personally without realizing that our corporate standing, the standing of the church of which we are a part, remains unaddressed.

Personal revival puts responsibility on the individual believer to bring his or her life in line with the Lordship of Christ. Corporate revival on the other hand puts heavy responsibility on the leadership of any Christian organization to bring their entity in line with the Lordship of Christ. The leaders must identify and resolve outstanding issues the *spiritual community* may have between itself and its Lord. An illustration of this in Israel's case was the high places they kept for worshipping idols. In a church it may involve a split, immorality by leaders in the past, faithless leadership, etc. Until these corporate failings get addressed by leadership, a ministry will find itself drained, prone to conflict and unfruitful, just as the nation of Israel found itself under similar divine discipline until they addressed their issues.

In the following section we'll review personal revival and move on to explore the focus of our attention, the revival of an entity. We'll also explore the lifecycle of a local church and what brings it to the place of needing corporate revival.

The Nature of Personal Revival

When we come to see that our heart has grown hard or indifferent toward the Lord, we embark on the path of personal revival. We may have drifted; we may have traded our love for the Lord for the pursuit of wealth, success or some other temporary sensual satisfaction; we may have settled for an outward expression of Christianity or become satisfied with a superficial cultural brand of Christianity. We may have added things to our routine that edge the Lord out of our daily life or have given in to a particular besetting sin. We may have become entangled in a relationship which we had no business pursuing in the first place or settled for a devotional life that resembles daily crumbs rather than daily bread. Maybe we have just become way too busy. That's when God often allows a crisis or tragedy to shake us out of our spiritually disastrous ways.

Tragedy and/or crises serve a dual purpose in our lives. They reveal what's in our heart and spur us back to the foundation of Christ. Trials—personal or corporate—become God's means to cause you to consider your need for revival. If, in God's mercy, He uses a trial to bring you to a place of realizing you've wandered from Him, you are not alone.

The Psalmist found himself at such a place in Psalm 119. The theme of Psalm 119 revolves around the word of God. We learn the benefits, the attributes and the effects of God's word. In addition, the Psalmist shares his attitude toward the word of God. He approaches it with his whole heart (vs. 2, 10, 34, 58, 69, 112, 145). He declares his love for the word (vs. 47, 97, 127, 159, and 167). He delights in the word and longs for and seeks opportunities to be in the word.

However, a secondary theme emerges from the heart of the author. What do you get when you combine an open-hearted approach to the word of God with a determination to spend time in His word? You get a heart cry for revival. The Psalmist's heart seeks personal revival throughout the stanzas of this song. He repeats one phrase nine times: "Revive me," "Revive me," "Revive me!" The KJV translates the phrase "Quicken me," and the NIV "Preserve me." *New life* is the idea that ties all those translations together, the addition of new spiritual stamina, new spiritual vitality. A whole-hearted love for and devotion to the word of God brings the Psalmist to the place where he cries out repeatedly, "Revive me"!

Listen to his heart:
> In verse 25: *"My soul cleaves to the dust; Revive me according to Thy word."*

In verse 37: *"Turn away my eyes from looking at vanity, and revive me in Thy ways."*

Verse 40: *"Behold I long for Thy precepts; Revive me through Thy righteousness."*

In verse 88 he says: *"Revive me according to Thy loving-kindness, So that I may keep the testimony of Thy mouth."*

Verse 107: *"I am exceedingly afflicted; Revive me, O LORD according to Thy word."*

Verse 149: *"Hear my voice according to Thy loving-kindness; Revive me, O LORD, according to Thine ordinances."*

In verses 154, 156 and 159: *"Plead my cause and redeem me; Revive me according to Thy word." "Great are Thy mercies, O LORD; Revive me according to Thine ordinances." "Consider how I love Thy precepts; Revive me, O LORD, according to Thy loving-kindness."*

How did the Psalmist become aware of his need for personal revival? What motivated him to cry out to God for this? It was the Holy Spirit working in his heart as he opened himself to the laser-like surgery of God's word. We can start down the path of personal revival by saturating ourselves in the word of God. As we do both our condition and need come into clear focus.

> "I have gone astray like a lost sheep; seek Thy servant."

The Psalmist declares his condition in the very last verse of Psalm 119. *"I have gone astray like a lost sheep; seek Thy servant."* When we realize that we have wandered away from God's sheep and from the Shepherd Himself, we also should cry out, "Revive me"! When the word of God exposes our inner lives and we suddenly see our condition as less than pleasing to the Lord, our Good Shepherd points us in the direction of personal revival.

The Nature of Corporate Sin and Revival

The corporate aspect of revival suffers neglect in our time but this has not always been the case. For example, in the Old Testament, godly leaders utilized Solemn Assemblies to call God's people corporately back to the Lord (see 1 Samuel 7; 1 Chronicles 13-16; 2 Chronicles 5-7; 2 Chronicles 15; 2 Chronicles 20; 2 Chronicles 23; 2 Chronicles 29; 2 Chronicles 34; Ezra 9-10; Nehemiah 8-9; Joel 1).[26] Solemn Assemblies are laid out in vivid detail in both Ezra and Nehemiah.

---

[26] Adapted from Richard Owen Roberts, *Sanctify the Congregation* (Wheaton, IL: International Awakening Press, 1994) 4-5.

Their primary purpose was to right the nation's relationship with God. Sin often infected the nation of Israel. When it did, the Lord held them accountable for their sin as a group. When sin finds a home amidst a group of New Testament believers, the Lord holds them corporately accountable just as He did in the Old Testament.

Corporate Sin

What do we mean by corporate sin? Corporate sin means sin a church commits acting as a group (such as an attitude of racism, or a split), or sin infecting the church without being treated (such as moral failure by lay or pastoral leadership). Here are a few biblical examples:

- The failure of the church at Corinth to discipline the man living in adultery was an indictment of the church itself. 1 Corinthians 5 was as much a call for the church's leaders to repent as it was for the individual living in sin. Anytime a church's leaders fail to listen to the Head about inappropriate things going on in the body, the church becomes accountable before God.

- Achan in Joshua 7 is another example of sin literally coming into the "camp." God held the entire group accountable for the hidden sin of one individual.

- Churches can also blunder into corporate behaviors they did not realize were sinful. Like Abimelech taking Sarah as a wife, churches can become guilty before God for taking action or failing to act without realizing God's opinion on the matter. In Abimelech's day it was culturally acceptable for a king to acquire many wives. But when Abimelech assimilated Sarah into his household, God held the entire kingdom accountable. Abimelech complains to God, *"Wilt thou slay an entire nation, even though blameless?"* He goes on to protest, *"In the integrity of my heart and the innocence of my hands I have done this"* (Genesis 20:1-18). Just like Abimelech, churches can assimilate the values of the culture around them and become guilty of corporate sin without conscious awareness of doing so.

- Similarly, corporate sin can take the form of not waiting on God. Joshua's failure to seek the Lord in regard to the Gibeonites caused the *nation* problems (Joshua 9). Years later the same incident led to a three year famine when Saul violated the Gibeonite covenant (2 Samuel 21). Churches too can fail to seek the Lord, taking matters into their own hands. It can happen without a second thought. Later they wonder where their sense of blessing has gone.

Much of corporate sin is tied to its leadership. Leaders set the pace and policy of the group, and, as those in authority, they become responsible before God for the response of the group. They will choose either to discipline, to tolerate, or to ignore sin in the body. A common path to sin spreading in the camp comes through leaders failing to implement church discipline. Such infections turn to cancer and then the surgery needed to remove the cancerous growth will be far more painful than the initial treatment would have been. If leaders fail to protect the body in this way, regaining their credibility can be slow going. It can shape the culture of the entire church and devastate its health for years.

> "If the leaders lead their people in a sinful direction or allow sin to be tolerated, the whole group becomes guilty."

If the leaders lead their people in a sinful direction or allow sin to be tolerated, the whole group becomes guilty. The congregation does not escape because they have merely followed flawed leadership. You cannot divorce a church's leadership from its followership. It is a *body*. Jesus looks at each church as a body, a functioning whole. Primary responsibility rests on church leaders, but the remaining members are infected and caught up in whatever discipline the Lord inflicts.

The culture of a church gets shaped by leaders' sinful decisions, and the spoken and unspoken values of the group influence their decisions. The interrelation of leaders, followers and a church's unique culture is strong, so strong that an individual in the congregation cannot say, "I am not tied to the corporate sin of my church." Our association with the church makes us share in its glories *and* its failures. When something great happens, we are quick to claim it as our own. "That's *my* church!" we say. When something bad goes down we cannot say, "*Those* leaders messed up." We must say, "*Our* leaders messed up and since I am a part of the body, I share responsibility for their actions." The letters to the churches in Revelation 2-3 make it clear there is collective responsibility for both the commendations *and* the condemnations the Lord gave.

Collective responsibility for sin shows up in different kinds of entities in Scripture. The Bible describes three types of corporate bodies; the local church, regional or denominational groups and nations. Each type is vulnerable to corporate sin. Each type has corporate revival available to it as well.

Corporate Revival on the Local Church Level

Our modern, westernized style of thinking has caused us to view most all of life through the lens of the individual. It may be foreign to us, but we need to accept that God holds *groups* of believers accountable. In Christ's seven letters to the churches in Revelation, each church received a unique message from Him and most got a call to corporate repentance! The Lord of the Church held each congregation accountable for what occurred among them. He has not changed. Roberts asks in relation to the seven churches: "If only two out of seven churches in the Revelation were not commanded to repent, what are the probabilities that your church is so pleasing to the Lord that He requires no repentance from you?"[27]

The seven letters have much to teach us. A church's deeds, doctrine and devotion come under the Lord's scrutiny. The Lord is immediately aware of everything transpiring in each of His congregations. He maintains a presence in each of these churches, for He walks among "*the lampstands.*"

What appears questionable is His blessing on some of them. Can He freely and fully bless a church like Pergamum that deviated from orthodox doctrine? What about a church that tolerated evil like Thyatira? To what extent can He bless a church which leaves behind the love they once had for Jesus as in the church at Ephesus? In each of these churches the congregations lost something important to Him. In one case it was their orthodoxy; in another it was their corporate purity; in the third they fell from their corporate love for Him. He will not fully bless them in this state.

The Apostle Paul asked the Galatian church: "*Where then is that sense of blessing you had?*" (Galatians 4:15 NASB) Something changed in their congregation. Something had been lost corporately. The NIV puts it: "*What has happened to all your joy?*" The Greek lines up with the NASB[28] but both versions communicate something significant had been lost.

In contrast, Matthew 18:20 says, "*For where two or three have gathered together in My name, there I am in their midst.*" This verse is often cited to assure us of the Lord's *presence* even when few are gathered in His name. But a *sense of blessing* is something else and *not* guaranteed. When we lack a sense of blessing in our

---

[27] Roberts, *Repentance*. 38.

[28] makarismos (blessing - see also Ro. 4:6,9 for similar usage) Walter Bauer, *A Greek English Lexicon of the New Testament and other Early Christian Literature* (Chicago, IL: University of Chicago Press, 1979) 487.

church, we are in dire need of corporate revival.

Corporate Revival on the Regional - Denominational Level

Taking the letters to the seven churches as a whole, we see the Lord addressing churches in a certain geographical area. They were all located in Asia Minor, within a hundred miles of each other. Is it too much of a stretch to believe the Lord is concerned with a geographic region's spiritual health? Jesus says, *"Write in a book what you see, and send it to 'the seven churches.'"* (Rev. 1:11) While Jesus addresses each church He also refers to them as a group. The word "seven" indicates a "denomination." The word "denomination" relates to numbers, just as the bills in your wallet are differentiated by their "denominations." The phrase, *"the seven churches,"* does not designate a "formal" denomination in the way we might imagine one organized today, yet we can still say Jesus is the Lord of the *Church* which includes any assortment of churches gathered in a specific "denomination." The various churches of Asia remain subject to His authority individually *and* as a group. Leaders of denominational entities bear responsibility for shepherding these larger scale flocks. The Lord wants to lead denominational leaders as much as He wants to lead leaders of a particular church.

Regional revival applies corporate revival to a larger scale than that of a local church. If regional denominational leaders stay close to the Lord and continue to be receptive to Him, they enjoy His blessing. However, whole movements can also become apostate that once were vibrant expressions of Christ. Have not many denominational groups declined and died spiritually? Would not the Lord speak to them about the condition of their assembly of churches as that decline occurred? Could He not also revive a denomination if they started listening to Him? The faith-filled answer is "Yes!" The effect could have a dramatic and far-reaching influence on our national spiritual climate.

Corporate Revival on the National Level

National revival occurred often in the Old Testament. Multiple cycles take place in the book of Judges alone. Several revivals are led by the kings of Israel and several more get facilitated by various prophets. All these occurred on a national stage and were corporate in nature. They took place among the people as a *nation*.

Israel though was established as a theocracy. Even kings reigned as "under shepherds" of God's overall reign. His covenant defined the relationship with His people as a nation. No other nation has this unique covenantal privilege, but that does not mean a nation cannot be blessed by God.

The United States has experienced God's blessing due to the heavy influence of evangelical Christianity in the settling of the colonies and birth of the nation. In the mid- 1800's, "Abraham Lincoln once called Americans 'the almost-chosen people.'"[29] For many years this nation enjoyed what might be termed a "Christian corporate consciousness."

Secularism's inroads and the Church's passivity have changed that in recent decades. Americans are not the "people of God" in the exact same way the Israelites were. But we have enjoyed significant national blessing for a time. What we can take from the example of national revivals in the history of Israel is this: A godly remnant amidst a decaying culture can set the process of revival in motion resulting in the re-blessing of a nation. It happened uniquely in Israel's history because of who they were, but a measure of that blessing can happen in ours or any nation when a majority of people listen to and follow what Jesus says.

In fact, several national revivals have occurred in America. Of course, not every person in the nation participated, but each revival grew to such proportions that it affected the nation as a whole—and blessed it!

Nobel Prize winner, Robert William Fogel, summarizes the cyclical nature of these national phenomena in his book, *The Fourth Great Awakening and The Rise of Egalitarianism*. He writes, "Upsurges in religious enthusiasm in America have tended to run in cycles lasting about one hundred years . . . These cycles overlay, the end of one cycle coinciding with the beginning of the next."[30] The cycles Fogel describes were of such magnitude that they were referred to as "Great Awakenings." They could just as well be labeled "National Awakenings." Each transformed the culture of their respective time periods. Each was unique in origin and effect. But all of them vastly improved the general spiritual health of the nation. Can we reach the national blessing point again? History says we may be ready for a new cycle!

Section Summary

The Bible shows that God works in both individuals and corporate entities in

---

[29] Mark A Wall, *The Puzzling Faith of Abraham Lincoln*, Christian History Magazine, Issue 33, Vol. XI, No. 1 as reported by Dawson 67

[30] Robert William Fogel, *The Fourth Great Awakening and the Future of Egalitarianism* (Chicago, IL: University of Chicago Press, 2000) 17.

revival. In corporate revival, God calls individual churches, groups of churches and even national bodies to become accountable to Him. He holds them accountable for their corporate condition and their history.

But one must ask: how does an entity, particularly a local church, find itself in need of corporate revival? A review of the lifecycle of a local church brings to light the causes of the church's hidden weaknesses.

Lifecycle of a Local Church

The lifecycle of a local church contains four recognizable phases. Those phases consist of 1) Growth, 2) Plateau, 3) Decline and 4) Death or Redevelopment. This is a pattern related to the aging of a congregation. A church, like a human being, is born, matures, declines and eventually dies. Denominations also follow a similar pattern, although they often take a long time to die organizationally. Let's examine each of these phases in detail.

Phase One - Growth

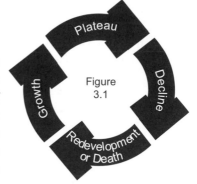

In the first phase of a church's lifecycle several characteristics accelerate the church's advancement. The planting and early years of most churches are generally challenging but exciting to the participants. God demonstrates His favor on the vision and passion of the church's founders. The clear sense of purpose and unifying values cultivate beautiful corporate synergy in healthy church starts. Often a high level of faith is exercised, as well as mutual cooperation and sacrifice.

The pioneering-types who start the church will often take "risks of faith" which God blesses. They develop innovative evangelistic outreaches. The result is an atmosphere of blessing. God moves and works because His people follow His lead. His people are flexible and responsive to opportunity. They often face obstacles but prayerfully seek God to reveal the opportunities within the obstacles. It's no wonder those involved in these early efforts will look back on these as "glory days," and feel spiritual longing and nostalgia. They were, in fact, glorious.

Phase Two - Plateau

At some point things begin to change as leaders begin to consolidate the gains made in the growth phase. Growth will require the increase of structure and organization to prevent chaos. This means the multiplication of programs and staff. The leaders start to lean on the machinery, and the faith required in those early days diminishes in the plateau phase. Decisions and direction slow down and become less flexible and innovative than before.

In the first phase it's as if the leaders are driving a speed boat, able to change directions in an instant if required; in the second phase, they run a cruise ship. Change becomes cumbersome and tricky. Subtly, the church's focus often changes from outward to inward, from evangelism to discipleship, from growth to maintenance. The synergy they once enjoyed begins to lag. Unity will often become challenged by crisis and conflict. If not led well during this phase, the "glory days" can turn into the "gory days." Like Israel in Judges, factions can arise within and without, straining the church in ways that limit God's blessing.
In place of the drama and excitement of the early days, "stability" and "security" become the new values. Now stability and security have their benefits. In many ways the plateau phase represents the church at its strongest. A stable church has the resources, which, if invested properly, can impact its community in ways a start-up church can only dream. If stability serves as a foundation for new challenges of faith and new opportunities to see God do amazing things, then stability becomes a blessing.

If, however, stability functions only to keep the corporate ship on an even keel and if the crew's only task becomes to keep the passengers happy, then the church starts taking on water without realizing it. Slow down and decline, though not immediate, become inevitable unless leaders do something to repair and restore power to the vessel.

Phase Three – Decline

To continue our analogy, if a ship takes on water, the weight of that water sends it in a direction (down!) it definitely did not set out to go. The crew finds itself expending its energy bailing or manning pumps. Sometimes bailing water becomes the goal, so that any effort to change the ship's course gets resisted by the weary but faithful crew. Though the captain may sense danger, the passengers do not fully grasp their peril . . . yet! If the captain does not himself jump ship anticipating the coming disaster, then he must help everyone face the crisis. He becomes even more preoccupied with safety procedures and calming the fears of passengers.

Keeping the machinery running, providing the programs, potlucks and entertainments scheduled to keep the passengers happy and somewhat sedated to the looming crisis becomes the focus of leadership. The passengers themselves want to be distracted from the slowing of the ship and rising water level during this period. Since it takes place over decades, most can't see the danger. Since the ship has not hit an iceberg or run aground, most continue in blissful ignorance of a problem. Meanwhile, rust perforates the hull and the seepage turns into leaks which become hard to stop. The sleek and swift speedboat becomes a memory.

Leakage during this phase of a church's lifecycle can create a "control" mentality where control replaces faith on the part of leadership. In essence leaders start "battening down the hatches." The ministry continues but filling leadership slots becomes more difficult and pastors/churches may lay hands on some too quickly during this phase. No one knows what the real problem is. The structure that functioned well when the church was large and stable begins to cause the ship to list to one side. Ministries and programs within the church begin to vie for increasingly limited resources. Morale sinks and infighting starts. Those who rock the boat may be placed in the brig or forced to walk the plank!

Phase Four – Redevelopment or Death

Declining numbers and resources, and the heightened anxiety these create, cause a church in the fourth phase of its lifecycle to face seemingly insurmountable obstacles to its survival. The church may continue for years in this phase. Worship services continue, the pastor preaches, and the board still meets month after month. Pastoral changes may transpire. Those who pioneered the work pass to their reward. Few are left who know the history of this great ship that was once the pride of their lives and community.

In this phase God may send a rescue ship to tow the listing vessel to port for a major overhaul. However, sometimes the life boats will be lowered for the few left, and the old ship, scuttled by the denomination or remaining leaders, sinks to the depths to become a parachurch ministry center or a restaurant.

Ship's Log

If we were to review this ship's log, we'd discover the church faced many challenges through the years and overcame them. Christ commends them for making it through each one. The glories of the church's history (which may be many) are recorded in His books. The Lord does not forget these good things but neither does He ignore the barnacles of sin that may have weighed it down through the years.

Close review of the logbook He kept as its true Captain shows that several times in the history of the church, He sounded alarms that went unheeded by the leadership under Him. If discerned properly, these alarms would have shown the church's leaders the true nature of their woes. Now, however, most of these leaders don't have the energy or interest to address the damage and repair it, much less grow the church. The denomination no longer has the patience or willingness to further subsidize the church's existence. The church's fate hangs in the balance. Will a younger pastor make a difference? A change in worship style maybe? Will navigating a different course solve the problem? Strands of hope or simple inertia hold the church together until a new wave of blessing comes or a final crisis brings the church to a close.

> "The decision to deal or not to deal with these issues usually determines whether the languishing local church will redevelop or will pass away."

The church usually experiences much corporate pain during its slow decline. Things such as splits, disunity, immoral conduct by leadership, power struggles and a highly combustible atmosphere can plague the church. Shallowness replaces the authentic fellowship a local church previously enjoyed. Such churches live on two levels: at one level, the church's leaders know these problems exist and suspect such problems hinder the church's ministry; on another level, they function as if the problems did not exist. They don't want to talk about them. Yet their shadow lingers over every decision they make.[31] The decision to deal or not to deal with these issues usually determines whether the languishing local church will redevelop or will pass away.

Corporate Epiphany

I have briefly made a case for the lifecycle of local churches. Here is the dilemma before us: The problems behind the cycles of revival in Israel's history were due to spiritual declension. The cycles of revival in American history resulted from God's people crying out in the midst of their spiritual decline. How can we fail to recognize that a local church may face the same spiritual decline before a revival?

---

[31] Dr. M. Scott Peck develops the concept of the organizational shadow in his book, *A World Waiting to be Born*. While I cannot endorse his theology, the veracity of his insights into corporate dysfunction is self-evident.

Dr. Harry Reeder writes in his book, *From Embers to a Flame*, ". . . in the history of a declining or dead church, there are almost always some things that were dead wrong – which means that the church is in need of repentance. This is not as depressing as it sounds, because it presents an opportunity for God to do a new and exciting work in the church . . . It may be that God has been withholding His blessing because the body has not repented, and when it does, He will open the floodgates and pour out His grace in unprecedented measure."[32]

If you are in a church where stability has now led to stagnation, can you consider the possibility that you are in spiritual decline? Are you willing to consider that your church may have a spiritual rather than program-related problem? If you find your church is in the fourth phase of a church's lifecycle and you have many unaddressed corporate crises in your history, are you willing to consider the possibility that, like Israel, God has your church under His discipline?

That admission is the first step to humbling ourselves, praying and crying out to God for revival. Until each local church's leadership takes responsibility for the spiritual health of the body under its charge, the pain and decline will continue. Our churches will go from difficulty to difficulty and from pain to pain until we grasp that the crises coming upon us are not accidental. God intends them to lead us all to humble ourselves, pray and seek His face. Then He can revive and heal us.

---

[32] Harry Reeder, *From Embers to a Flame*, (Phillipsburg NJ: P&R Publishing 2004) 37-38

Chapter Four

If my people ...
will humble themselves

"But what we do need to do is to humble ourselves before God, and seek the fullness, the direction and the power of the Holy Spirit. For then our churches will at least come close to the essentials of a living church in Apostolic doctrine, loving fellowship, joyful worship and outgoing, ongoing evangelism."
— John Stott

Consider this great story of corporate revival in a local church. In the spring of 1890,

> ". . . the United Brethren Church was sadly divided on the secrecy question,[33] and in many places two pastors were employed – one by the "Liberals" and another by the "Radicals" of the same congregation. In our travels we stopped to visit an old friend, who was the "Radical" pastor in such a place as these to whom we have referred . . . Sunday evening our friend invited us to preach for him. God gave us unusual liberty in prayer and in preaching His word, and opened the very windows of heaven, and showers of blessing fell upon that dry and barren land. In spite of circumstances so utterly forbidding, in one short hour, the people found themselves in the midst of a powerful revival. We never witnessed so much confession in so short a time. Many in tears asked each other's forgiveness, and then came to the altar together, and prayed that they might regain their first love; and God heard and answered their prayers.

---

[33] The secrecy question revolved around the issue of whether or not church members could also belong to secret societies such as the Masons.

The "Liberal" pastor was not present, but the "Liberal" presiding-elder was; and he and the "Radical" pastor had had little confidence in each other; but under the mighty power of the Spirit, their hearts were united, and they embraced each other in tears. Thus did God manifest His power, and get to His own name glory; and to Him alone be praise, both now and forever, for in His hands are the hearts of the children of men." [34]

Can you imagine a local church so divided that each camp within the church had its own pastor? They lived together as a split church under the same roof! The account of this revival under the ministry of S.B. Shaw demonstrates the importance of humility to activate revival. It also shows the way revival itself generates humility among those who experience it. The congregation's tears, confession and seeking forgiveness displayed their brokenness and humility before God. With that brokenness came an eager willingness to reconcile with their brothers with whom they were in conflict. The humility they showed to reconcile with God engendered humility and reconciliation among men. The account of this revival fleshes out the part humility plays in the re-blessing of a local church as seen in 2 Chronicles 7:14, *"If my people . . . will humble themselves."*

This call to humility suggests God's people have issues over which they *need* to humble themselves. The conditional nature of the promise assumes that God's people had, to that point, failed to *recognize* their need to humble themselves, perhaps resisting it entirely. It finally suggests that, without humility, the remaining conditions of 2 Chronicles 7:14 (prayer, seeking His face and turning from wicked ways) are unlikely. This summons for God's people to humble themselves is the first condition of revival and the foundation upon which the others rest.

Humbling Realizations

If the people of Israel needed to humble themselves to experience a renewal of God's blessing, what kept them from doing so in the first place? More importantly, what keeps *us* from humbling *ourselves*?

We often fail to humble ourselves because we misdiagnose the world's problems. We see things deteriorating in society and recognize the need for a spiritual awakening. We might even pray along those lines. We may witness the signs of divine discipline on our nation. But we fail to recognize this moral decline

---

[34] S. B. Shaw, *Touching Incidents and Remarkable Answers to Prayer* (Chicago: S. B. Shaw, Publisher, 1897) 225.

indicates the *Church's* spiritual sickness, not the nation's alone. Roberts writes, "As soon as it becomes evident that immorality is on the increase and spirituality is on the decline, the biblically sound and spiritually lively Church will not foolishly blame the world but will immediately recognize its own complicity. The Church must first repent, for the righteous judgment was not against the world but against the church. Therefore in times of spiritual declension and moral decadence, the great duty of every Christian is both to discover those sins which have caused the judgment and to put them away . . . ."[35]

The symptoms show up in the culture, but the illness lies squarely in the heart of the Church. Spiritual deficiencies in the Body of Christ have led to our national moral crises. Now *that's* humbling. We need to assume responsibility for our sickness with humility, otherwise revival will continue to prove elusive.

Writing from a Birmingham jail cell, Dr. Martin Luther King Jr. penned, "There was a time when the church was very powerful – in the time when the early Christians rejoiced at being deemed worthy to suffer for what they believed. The church was not merely a thermometer that recorded the ideas and principles of popular opinion; it was a thermostat that transformed the mores of society."[36]

So, how are we doing with that? Do you feel the Church in America reflects the "ideas and principles of popular opinion" or does it "transform the mores of society?" When the answer is closer to the former rather than the latter, we must face the fact that the root of society's ills resides in the heart of the Church. Until we accept that premise we will not see the need to humble ourselves. We may pray for our nation; we may pray for revival, but the humility God seeks among His people will be scarce. As long as we blame society or a political party or teenagers or whoever for the moral decline, the Church's ill-health, *our* church's ill-health, goes overlooked. When we ignore the real roots of our culture's spiritual sickness, the call for humility sounds foreign to us.

The Lord put these words in the mouth of the prophet Hosea: "*Though I wrote for him ten thousand precepts of My law, they are regarded as a strange thing.*" (Hosea 8:12). The Israelites just did not get it. What the prophet told them sounded foreign to their ears. They failed to see the relevance. They had gone so deep into idolatry that, when God reminded them of His precepts, they in essence replied: "What in the world are you talking about?" They did not see

---

[35] Roberts, *Sanctify the Congregation* 9.
[36] Martin Luther King Jr. Papers Project, *Letters from a Birmingham Jail* http://www.stanford.edu/group/king/popular_requests/frequentdocs/birmingham.pdf

their sin for what it was. Their perception of their condition was miles from God's perception!

We'd all like to believe that, if the Lord revealed our shortcomings, either corporate or personal, we would repent and immediately deal with what He reveals. The truth is we do everything we can to avoid facing the reality of our failures and shortcomings. Rationalizations, denial, projecting our faults on others, and blaming the devil are a few of the mechanisms we employ to avoid the light of God's word shining with conviction into our hearts. We assume such messages are not meant for us. It sounds to us like a *strange thing*." It often takes God sending divine discipline—personally or corporately—to get our attention, sometimes repeatedly, sometimes with greater and more devastating pain. It takes the Holy Spirit giving us a new angle of insight. Apart from such influences we just don't get the message.

> "It often takes God sending divine discipline – personally or corporately – to get our attention..."

Perceptual Disparity

To be humbled we must be willing to consider a *disparity* between the way we see ourselves and the way God sees us. "Disparity" speaks of inequality or incongruity. Perceptual disparity means a significant difference exists in the way two parties observe the same subject. Their viewpoints don't line up. Given the moral climate of our nation, it is likely that local churches fail at this very moment to see themselves the way the Lord of the Church sees them. Entire denominations would also share this distorted view.

Why humble ourselves if we believe that God views us favorably? Are we convinced the opinion we hold of our church is 100% consistent with God's opinion? We must be open to the possibility that a gap may exist between our perception and God's. God's view of us is the true view. A gap in perception stems from our own fallible, sin-smeared eyesight. Humility starts when we become open to the possibility that our perspective is flawed and can't bring our true state into focus.

The following four quadrants illustrate the fallibility of human perception (Figure 4.1). There can be degrees of perceptual disparity between each of the four quadrants. The same disparities may exist between the way we view ourselves and the way God views us personally or on a denominational level.

Quadrant A: The Way A Church Sees Itself

How does a church develop a corporate self-perception in the first place? How do they come to view themselves the way they do? Corporate self-perception can be based on any number of factors.

Some churches define their identity theologically, by a particular model of systematic theology (such as Reformed) while another may choose a different systematic framework (such as Dispensational). Whatever the framework, such churches primarily define their existence in terms of protecting, maintaining and promoting a particular approach to the Scriptures.

Other churches define themselves by their governance structure or their denominational affiliation, or perhaps by their *lack* of denominational affiliation (i.e. "Independent" Baptist or Bible churches). Some churches are defined by their message. They see distinctives in their message that set them apart from other bodies of believers. These distinctives become the reason for their existence.

Missions, the deeper life, or social justice may define the church in the minds of congregants. Some churches define themselves in terms of their ministry model. Cell churches, seeker-sensitive churches, and program-driven models become part of the very mentality of the church that bases its identity on how it does ministry.

Four Ways of Seeing a Church: [37]

The Way a Church Sees Itself (Quadrant A)	**The Way Others See a Church** (Quadrant B)
The Way a Church Thinks Others See It (Quadrant C)	**The Way God Sees a Church** (Quadrant D)

Figure 4.1

---

[37] The Four Ways of Seeing a Church is adapted from the Johari window developed by Joseph Luft and Harry Ingham in 1955.

A church can also define itself positively by its strong attendance figures or negatively by the lack thereof. In some cases the church's vision becomes the hallmark of their self-perception. You may hear churches say they want to be "multicultural" or "a church that reaches families," or "a church geared to the urban population," or "a church that targets the emerging generation" or "a traditional church." Take your pick of identity statements.

A church may see itself as a combination of several of these attributes. The values, stated or unstated, a church embraces create a corporate self-perception in the minds of both its leaders and members.

Quadrant B – How Others See a Church

This quadrant represents how those outside the local church view it. Such perceptions may be developed by something as innocuous as the condition of the church's property, signage, things they have heard from others or their own limited experiences with the church. If a church manages to serve its community well, it may enjoy a positive perception by those outside. If it has instead a long history of conflict or internal failures, these will also go into outsiders' perception of the church. It is likely that their perception will differ from those inside the church. The variant perspectives depend on different sources of information about the church.

Quadrant C – The Way a Church Thinks Others See It

A church's leadership and membership make assumptions about how people perceive it in the community. Surveying the community around one's church to discover what perceptions exist will open eyes to the reality. Lacking such accurate information, the church has to assume what others think. If your church is not growing, the reason may be found in the actual perception of the community about your church. A delusion in the way a church *thinks* people see it and the way people *actually* see it prevents a church from recognizing why they might need to humble themselves.

Quadrant D – The Way God Sees a Church

How does God look at your church? What factors does He use to develop His perception of a local body of believers? For answers to these questions we go to the seven letters to the churches in Revelation 2-3. There we discover that the Lord Jesus consistently used three instruments of measure to determine His view of a particular body of believers: deeds, devotion, and doctrine.

Deeds

The first measure the Lord uses in assessing a church is its deeds. Jesus told the church at Ephesus, "*I know your deeds . . .*" He calls them to reflect on their behavior and "*do the deeds you did at first or else I am coming to you and will remove your lampstand . . .*" (Revelation 2:2, 5). He said to the church at Thyatira, "*I know your deeds . . . and that your deeds of late are greater than at first*" (Revelation 2:19). To the church at Sardis Jesus said, "*I know your deeds, that you have a name that you are alive but you are dead . . . I have not found your deeds completed in the sight of My God*" (Revelation 3:1-2). To the congregation at Philadelphia He writes, "*I know your deeds. Behold, I have set before you an open door which no one can shut, because you have a little power, and have kept My word, and have not denied My name*" (Revelation 3:8). And to Laodicea Jesus says, "*I know your deeds, that you are neither cold nor hot . . .*" (Revelation 3:15).

Deeds from the Lord's perspective are not only associated with "good works" as we define them. Each letter broadens the meaning of a church's deeds to include a wide range of behaviors. In some cases "deeds" refer to the *lack* of certain appropriate behaviors. A church's deeds specifically refer to their conduct, their action or inaction in any given situation.

Devotion

The second measure the Lord uses to assess a local church is a church's devotion. Jesus says to the Ephesian church, "*But I have this against you, that you have left your first love*" (Revelation 2:4). Jesus encourages the believers of Smyrna to be faithful when tested: "*Be faithful until death, and I will give you the crown of life*" (Revelation 2:10). To the church at Pergamum Jesus says, "*I know where you dwell, where Satan's throne is; and you hold fast My name, and did not deny My faith, even in the days of Antipas, My witness, My faithful one, who was killed among you, where Satan dwells*" (Revelation 2:13). Jesus emphasizes the importance of devotion when He writes to the Philadelphia church, "*Because you have kept the word of My perseverance, I also will keep you from the hour of testing, that hour which is about to come upon the whole world, to test those who dwell upon the earth*" (Revelation 3:10). Finally, the waning devotion of the church at Laodicea receives His rebuke: "*Because you say, 'I am rich and have become wealthy, and have need of nothing.' And you do not know that you are wretched and miserable and poor and blind and naked*" (Revelation 3:17).

Devotion thus goes beyond the deeds a church does to the secret thoughts and intents in the heart of a church. It includes the Laodicean's not-so-humble estimation of themselves. His measure of our devotion evaluates unseen values, attitudes, commitment, and fidelity of a church to Him. He searches the hearts and minds of people who gather in His name to discern the truth about this.

Doctrine

Doctrine is the third measure the Lord uses to evaluate a local congregation. Jesus commended the Ephesian church, ". . . *you cannot endure evil men, and you put to the test those who call themselves apostles, and they are not and you found them to be false*" (Revelation 2:2). The Lord found fault with the church at Pergamum because of their toleration of some among them who held "*the teaching of Balaam, who kept teaching Balak to put a stumbling block before the sons of Israel, to eat things sacrificed to idols and commit acts of immorality. Thus you also have some who in the same way hold the teaching of the Nicolaitians*" (Revelation 3:14-15). Doctrinal problems also show up in the church at Thyatira: "*But I have this against you, that you tolerate the woman Jezebel, who calls herself a prophetess, and she teaches and leads My bond-servants astray, so that they commit acts of immorality and eat things sacrificed to idols*" (Revelation 2:20).

Accurate Scriptural teaching was not to be hijacked by any individual with strange ideas. Doctrine was important to the Lord of the Church and served as part of the basis for His evaluation of it.

So we see that the Lord looks at a church from three angles to develop His perception of them. Deeds, devotion and doctrine bring a congregation's standing into clear focus before the Lord. He critiques the churches of Revelation based on the choices and events that transpired in the *history* of each church. He does not pull His perceptions out of thin air, nor are they based on mere supposition or opinion. Jesus uses hard evidence from each church's history to paint the accurate spiritual picture of all seven congregations (See Figure 4.2 below).

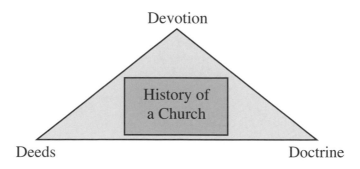

Appraisal Gap

Having explored the angles from which Jesus appraises a church and the nature of the four quadrants from Figure 4.1, the problem with perceptual disparity becomes clear. The way a church views itself (Quadrant A) and the way others view the church (Quadrant B) can be miles apart. Perceptual disparity can also be found between how a church views itself (Quadrant A) and how it thinks others view the church (Quadrant C). A church could be in for a wake up call if it thinks all is well with the neighboring community only to discover that the neighbors find something offensive in the life of the church of which the church itself is blissfully unaware.

This leads us to the question of utmost importance. Can there be disparity between the way a church views itself (Quadrant A) and the way God views the same church (Quadrant D)? In this Age of Grace, it may seem hard to fathom that God views our church less kindly than we might. But we may define our church's identity in ways that have nothing in common with the way Jesus appraises us. Several of the churches Jesus addressed in Revelation 2 and 3 were doubtless shocked to discover the gap between their corporate self-perception and Jesus' appraisal of them.

This appraisal gap existed between God and the Israelites in the Old Testament. Isaiah 58:1-9 demonstrates this:

> "Cry loudly, do not hold back; Raise your voice like a trumpet, and declare to My people their transgressions, and to the house of Jacob their sins. Yet they seek Me day by day, and delight to know My ways, as a nation that has done righteousness, and has not forsaken the ordinance of their God. They ask Me for just decisions, they delight in the nearness of God. 'Why have we fasted and Thou dost not see? Why have we humbled ourselves and Thou dost not notice?'
>
> Behold, on the day of your fast you find your desire, and drive hard all your workers. Behold, you fast for contention and strife and to strike with a wicked fist. You do not fast like you do today to make your voice heard on high. Is it a fast like this which I choose, a day for a man to humble himself? Is it for bowing one's head like a reed and for spreading out sackcloth and ashes as a bed? Will you call this a fast, even an acceptable day to the LORD?
>
> Is this not the fast which I choose, to loosen the bonds of wickedness, to undo the bands of the yoke, and to let the oppressed go free and break every yoke?

Is it not to divide your bread with the hungry and bring the homeless poor into the house; when you see the naked, to cover him; and not to hide yourself from your own flesh?

Then your light will break out like the dawn, and your recovery will speedily spring forth; and your righteousness will go before you; the glory of the LORD will be your rear guard. Then you will call, and the LORD will answer; you will cry, and He will say, 'Here I am.' If you remove the yoke from your midst, the pointing of the finger and speaking wickedness . . ."

The Israelites of Isaiah's time saw themselves as people who sought the Lord "*day by day*." They claimed they had "*done righteousness*" and acted as if they had "*not forsaken the ordinances of their God*." They felt they delighted "*to know God's ways*." They fasted and humbled themselves. But their prayers went unanswered because God had a very different appraisal of their standing than they had of themselves. They were not even conscious of the problems God articulates. For instance, they failed to see any difficulty with the way they treated their workers. They went through the motions of humbling themselves, even of fasting, but they were clueless about the way their actions offended God.

If they deal with the issues God has with them, He promises the restoration of health, answered prayer, righteousness, and the return of God's glory. Do you find it possible that God might see your church in a manner other than the way you perceive? Could we be as blind as those who lived in Isaiah's day? Surely not! Well perhaps . . .

Disparity on Display

Perhaps you've heard about the story of the "Emperor's New Clothes." A self-absorbed royal wanted the best of everything, but gets sold a bill of invisible goods. He parades through town in his transparent garb unaware of his need for sunscreen. Everyone goes along with the delusion. Only when a child speaks out does the emperor suddenly realize his "exposure" to ridicule.

Have you heard the true story about the "Church that Had No Clothes?" An entire congregation thinks they are clothed with the finest fabrics their money can buy but before Christ they parade around in their birthday suits! Jesus tells the church at Laodicea: "*Because you say, 'I am rich and have become wealthy, and have need of nothing', and **you do not know** that you are wretched and miserable and poor and blind and **naked** . . .*" (Revelation 3:17). Not only were the Laodiceans naked, they were unaware of their nakedness!

Is it possible we are blind about our corporate standing before God? The more self-assured we feel, the more distant from God we may be! The Laodiceans' overconfidence left them blindsided by His rebuke. He described their condition so our churches could learn! (See Figure 4.3 below.)

How the Laodicean church saw itself:	How God saw the Laodicean church:
"I am rich"	"you are wretched"
"and have become wealthy"	"and miserable"
"and have need of nothing"	"and poor and blind and naked"

How could a local church have an opinion of itself so diametrically opposed to the opinion God had of them? They thought they were rich, the Lord thought they were wretched. They thought they were wealthy, the Lord thought they were miserable. They thought they had no needs, the Lord said they were poor and blind and naked! We're not talking about Old Testament believers who did not have the indwelling Holy Spirit. This is a church during the glory days of the First Century! Can we honestly look at our church and confidently say that God has no issue with us? Whose church then is in need of revival?

> "We must start doubting our own perceptions to be willing to go to the Lord for *His* insight."

We see why we must humble ourselves, admit the prospect that the Lord may see our church differently and seek His viewpoint. Wilberforce writes, "We need to see our true state as God sees it. Because of His perfect purity and His ability to know us better then we know ourselves, it is likely that he sees problems and failures we are barely conscious of – if we recognize them at all. Over time, our defense systems have the ability to dull the conviction of the acts and attitudes that violate God's holiness. Remorse can turn to faint recognition. But God still knows those actions in the now."[38]

Double Vision

Usually when we read a book we hope things will be clearer for having done so. But in order for us to begin to see things from God's perspective, our current

---

[38] Wilberforce 166.

"clarity" must be challenged. The confidence with which we presently think about our church must be released. We must start doubting our own perceptions to be willing to go to the Lord for His insight. How do we do this? Consider the following possibility of corporate "double vision."

Local churches acquire certain traditions, viewpoints, values and ways of relating to each other. These behaviors get modeled by the leadership and the rest of the congregation mirrors those traits. These form the "culture" of your church. We generally put this culture on display before the visitors who show up on Sunday morning.

But every church also has a *subculture*. A subculture consists of the attitudes, behaviors and kinds of relating that go on behind the scenes in different groups. The subculture of a church is harder to define. But in some churches a kind of "double vision" develops where the subculture and the Sunday morning culture are at odds with each other. In truth it's not long before an unhealthy subculture infects the spirit of the Sunday morning culture. (Visitors sense the stifled spirit within minutes.)

The job of church leaders is to be concerned about the true state of the church's health. When it's healthy, the task can be difficult but rewarding. In a healthy church, leaders function together, using their gifts in ways that benefit the entire body. When healthy, leaders demonstrate freedom and spontaneity, enjoying harmony in their relationships with other leaders. They may still experience tension with each other but deal with their tension in a healthy way. The tension facilitates greater creativity and dependence on the Lord to lead them. In healthy churches a minimum of disparity exists between the church's subculture and its positive Sunday morning persona.

When a church's health is poor, real problems lurk behind the scenes and leaders may be at a loss to know what to do about it. They carry on from week to week until something *else* painful happens that reminds them the church is not right. For those of you in church leadership, would you feel free to describe to a visitor how your church actually operates behind the scenes?

If you are a member of the congregation and not in leadership, do you sense it is okay to ask your leaders how things operate behind the scenes? If not, that in itself might be a clue to a lack of integrity in the heart of your church. My goal is not to create suspicion but simply to demonstrate the possibility that things are not always what they seem. All of us who love the Church and serve its purposes want the Body of Christ to be healthy. We are sometimes surprised by how unhealthy things really are. If your church is sick, leaders will know and experience it, just as your head knows when your body is sick. They may not know why, but there is no doubt about the experience of corporate illness. If your church is healthy, there will be an inner resonance with the identity and vision your church projects.

If one is aware that disparity exists between the public and private culture of one's church, you know the Lord is aware of it. When the Lord evaluates a church, is His perception based only on what we do on Sunday morning? Hardly. We need to see what He sees. Only the Lord can cure our "double vision" and imprecise self-evaluation, but that will never happen unless we humble ourselves before Him.

The Danger of Not Humbling Ourselves

In Jeremiah's day, the Scripture says of God's people: "'*But they have not become contrite even to this day, nor have they feared nor walked in My law or My statutes, which I have set before you and before your fathers. Therefore thus says the LORD of hosts, the God of Israel, 'Behold, I am going to set My face against you for woe, even to cut off all Judah'*" (Jeremiah 44:10-11).

If we do not humble ourselves, it leads God to radically alter His disposition toward us. Some might be tempted to dismiss Jeremiah 44:10-11 as an Old Testament relic, but they should consider Revelation 2:5: "*Remember therefore from where you have fallen, and repent and do the deeds you did at first; or else I am coming to you and will remove your lampstand out of its place – unless you repent.*" The local church that refuses to humble itself faces a line God places in the sand. We may unknowingly cross it, and then God's discipline turns to destruction.

An ardent supporter of the First Great Awakening, a pastor named Thomas Foxcroft, entered his pulpit on July 30th 1724 and delivered a message titled, *God's Face Set against an Incorrigible People*. He preached on Jeremiah 44:10-11 and made the following declaration:

> "If a people are finally impenitent, God will thus set His face against them for evil. He may bear long with them but He will not bear always. He is a gracious and longsuffering God, but if His patience is abused and His grace turned into wantonness, it will kindle His anger and He will punish at the last. If a professing people forsake the Lord, then He will turn and will do them hurt,

after that He had done them good. If they finally forsake God, He will be angry with them until He consumes them utterly." [39]

We do not hear messages like that today, but perhaps we don't need them. We all know that evangelical churches are healthy, vibrant entities free of problems and dysfunction, right? Thank goodness we don't need to worry about such things! We likely feel our church would be similar to one of the two churches in Revelation 2-3 that Jesus commends without criticism.

We forget in our day what James told believers in his day: *"Be miserable and mourn and weep; let your laughter be turned into mourning and your joy to gloom. Humble yourselves in the presence of the Lord, and He will exalt you"* (James 4:9-10). Leonard Ravenhill's words ring out, "The so-called evangelical church is in trouble . . . Could it be that right now we need a mighty *baptism of honesty* in the Church – a mighty bending of the knees and breaking of the heart to admit that we are sleeping on the job?"[40] (Italics mine.) Are you convinced that the way *you* see your church is the way *God* sees your church? In this critical hour may God grant us a fresh baptism of honesty. *"If my people who are called by my name* **will humble themselves . . . !"**

---

[39] Roberts, *Sanctify the Congregation* 184.
[40] Leonard Ravenhill, *America is too Young to Die* (Minneapolis, MN: Bethany Fellowship Inc., 1979) 106.

Chapter Five

If my people ...
will pray

"Where are the prayer groups, where are the companies of intercessors, where are the churches that are united in an agonizing cry that God would open the heavens and come down and cause the mountains of hindrance and sin and unbelief to melt before his presence? There is only one thing that will save us in this hour of desperation and that is prayer."
- Stephen Olford

Could it be that God waits on us to pray before He sends a fresh blessing from above? Could it be that, by humbling ourselves and praying, He prepares us for the blessing we long to see? Is it really that simple? Simple – maybe. Easy – no! A.W. Tozer once observed that revivals are "born after midnight." He suggested that the stirring of the heart towards revival leads us into protracted periods of prayer. Additionally, those who *labor* in pray for revival may be misunderstood by others who do not feel the same hunger pains for God's blessing. Tozer writes,

"Occasionally there will appear on the religious scene a man whose unsatisfied spiritual longings become so big and important in his life that they crowd out every other interest. Such a man refuses to be content with the safe and conventional prayers of the frost-bound brethren who 'lead in prayer' week after week and year after year in the local assemblies. His yearnings carry him away and often make something of a nuisance out of him. His puzzled fellow Christians shake their heads and look knowingly at each other, but like the blind man who cried after his sight and was rebuked by the disciples, he 'cries the more a great deal.' And if he has not yet met the conditions or there is something hindering the answer to his prayer, he may pray on into the late hours. Not the hour of night but the state of his heart decides the time of his visitation. For him it may well be that revival comes after midnight."[41]

By way of comparison we have to ask: are we persevering enough? Are we desperate enough? Are we so dissatisfied with our spiritual ill health that we willingly and completely give ourselves to prayer for new blessing? Is our church tired enough of its treadmill activities that we are ready to bend the knee and keep it bent until God brings us to the blessing point? Does our disgust with the state of the world and what it suggests about the health of the Church light the fuse of prayer in us for the Holy Spirit's outpouring? This is the only path of revival available. God used insatiable spiritual hunger expressed through prayer to ignite every great revival this nation has witnessed. It waits to be seen if it will stir in us again.

Prayer and the Evangelical Awakening in England

John Wesley wrote in his journal,

> "While at Oxford, my brother and I and two more agreed to spend three or four evenings a week together. Our plan was to read over the classics on week nights and on Sunday some book on theology. . . Soon after, one of our company, now five persons, told us that he had been much abused the day before for being a member of the 'The Holy Club.' It had become a common topic of mirth at his college, where they accused us of customs which we did not do."[42]

This "Holy Club" is seen as one of the forerunners of the Evangelical Awakening. It led to a movement of revival and evangelism that swept through England and America in the mid 1700s.

Some humbling realizations stand out about this small band that gathered for study, good works and spiritual advancement. The most glaring is that the Wesley brothers—John and Charles—were only nominal Christians at the time. They had not yet come to know the Lord as Savior. Their experience of God was limited to the religious interests of the day. They were not praying for revival but sought to please God by putting the Scriptures into the best practice they knew how. Prayer was one of their disciplines to satisfy divine requirements.[43]

---

[41] AW Tozer, *Born after Midnight* (Harrisburg PA: Christian Pub. 1959) 8-9.
[42] Clare George Weakley, *The Nature of Revival* (Minneapolis: Bethany House 1987) 21-22.
[43] Weakley 26.

How astounding that God started with people outside the realm of saving faith! Yet their spiritual hunger, when He finally satisfied it, led ultimately to a glorious advancement of His kingdom! If we who know the Lord hesitate to draw near for fresh blessing, the hearts of those who as yet do not know Him may be stirred to do so! The story of the "Holy Club" both encourages and warns us. It encourages us in that God took a small group of willing hearts and worked mightily in them. Through those same willing hearts He raised up a movement that brought dramatic increase into the Kingdom of God and transformed society.

The warning of the "Holy Club" should sober the Church and its churches. If the Church proves less than responsive to her Lord, He may raise up other servants outside present denominations to lead new movements that *will* respond to Him. The "Holy Club" and the Awakening that followed began in a day eerily similar to our own. Historian W.H. Fitchett writes of England's moral decline in the early 18th century,

> "Its ideals were gross; its sports were brutal; its public life was corrupt, its vice was unashamed . . . foulness stained the general speech. Judges swore on the bench; . . . the king swore incessantly . . . Justice itself was cruel. It was the age of . . . the whipping post . . . and of the debtor's prisons . . . Drunkenness was the familiar and unrebuked habit . . . Adultery was a sport. . ." [44]

Thomas Secker, the Bishop of Oxford wrote in 1739 describing the general disdain for Christianity during the same period:

> "In this we cannot be mistaken, that an open and professed disregard of religion is become, through a variety of unhappy causes, the distinguishing character of the age . . . Christianity is ridiculed and railed at with very little reserve; and the teacher of it without any at all." [45]

John Wesley denounced the state of the Church in England with these words,

> "Look east, west, north or south, name what parish you please, is Christian fellowship there? Rather are not the bulk of the parishioners a mere rope of sand? What Christian connection is there between them? What intercourse in spiritual things? What watching over each other's souls?" [46]

---

[44] W. H. Fitchett, *Wesley and His Century* (New York, NY: Eaton and Mains, 1906) 139-140.

[45] Poteur and Stinton, *The Works of Thomas Secker Vol. V.* Quoted by A. Sivington Wood. *The Inextinguishable Blaze; Spiritual Renewal and Advance in the Eighteenth Century.* (Grand Rapids, MI: Eerdmans Publishing) 16.

[46] Fitchett 220.

The age in which the Wesley's lived was one of moral decline, cold spirituality and public disdain for the Church. Sound familiar? If God had not intervened by raising up a small band of college students meeting together for the betterment of their souls, who knows into what state the world would have declined and what conditions the following generations would have inherited?

Prayer and the First Great Awakening in America

As Europe's Evangelical Awakening made its way to America, the movement faced the same hard ground in New England that was found in England. The Church wallowed in formality and tradition. It lacked spontaneity and spiritual vitality. The First Great Awakening, however, sent an electric shock through the body of Christ in America. Commentary on the revival comes from the history written of one Presbyterian Church in Basking Ridge, New Jersey.

> "Concerning this tremendous religious revival which spread at this time from Massachusetts to Georgia, there was a great difference of opinion and much argument, especially among the clergy. Some people were apparently much offended by the 'harsh, uncharitable spirit with which they were denounced and misrepresented by the preachers.' Some felt that the meetings tended to arouse too much emotional excitement rather than a spiritual awakening. But Dr. Alexander in his book, '*The Log College*,' wrote that at this period 'the Presbyterian Church in America was in a most deplorable state of deadness and formality; and that the necessity of a change of heart was very little inculcated from the pulpit, or understood by the people.'" [47]

How did prayer break through the spiritual deadness and religious formality in America? Consider the most famous sermon of the time, "*Sinners in the Hands of an Angry God*," by Jonathan Edwards. It acts as a reference point for the work God did in the First Great Awakening. There is a story behind Edward's famous message that's seldom told:

> "All the world has heard how the audience of the elder President Edwards was moved by his terrible sermon on 'Sinners in the hands of an angry God;' some of them even grasping hold of the pillars of the sanctuary, from the feeling that their feet were actually sliding into the pit. But the secret of that sermon's power is known to but few. Some Christians in the vicinity (Enfield, Mass.) had become alarmed, lest, while God was blessing other places, He should in anger pass them by; and so they met on the preceding evening and spent the

---

[47] McFadden, Van Dyke and Johnston, *The Presbyterian Church* Basking Ridge, NJ A History 6.

whole night in agonizing prayer."[48]

During the First Great Awakening, at least one group of laypeople, moved by desperation, prayed for God's intervention. They did not want to be passed by! This unknown group of individuals called down God's anointing and it showed up on the preacher the next morning. Jonathan Edward's famous message was anointed to such a degree that people still read and study the sermon today. Listening to a rendition of Edward's sermon, one notices its intellectual weight and serious tone. Without the anointing of the Holy Spirit though, it would seem a dry lecture. With agonizing prayer and God speaking powerfully though His messenger, it turned out to be one of the fuses that lit the fire of the First Great Awakening. Prayer by a small group of unnamed individuals paved the way.

Prayer and the Revival of 1857 - 1858

The flame of revival was again lit on Fulton Street in New York City in the Fall of 1857. One freshly minted, unassuming, inner city missionary burdened for evangelism did something inspired. Instead of immediately going about to spread the Gospel, he called for a prayer meeting. Edwin Orr recounts the details of the story,

> "Burdened by the need, Jeremiah Lanphier decided to invite others to join him in a noonday prayer-meeting, to be held once a week on Wednesdays. Accordingly, at twelve noon, 23 September 1857, the door was opened and the faithful Lanphier took his seat to await the response to his invitation. Five minutes went by. No one appeared. The missionary paced the room in a conflict of fear and faith. Ten minutes elapsed. Still no one came. Fifteen minutes passed. Lanphier was yet alone. Twenty minutes; twenty-five; thirty; and then at twelve-thirty p.m. a step was heard on the stairs, and the first person appeared, then another, and another, and another, until six people were present and the prayer-meeting began . . . Within six months 10,000 businessmen gathered daily in New York City for prayer and within two years, a million converts had been added to the American churches."[49]

One million converts in two years! Now keep in mind that the entire population of the United States in 1858 was 30,000,000.[50] That represents over 3% of the population being brought to Christ. In today's numbers that would bring an

---

48 Shaw, *Touching Incidents and Remarkable Answers to Prayer* 153.
49 J. Edwin Orr, *The Second Great Awakening* (London: Marshall, Morgan & Scott, 1949) 16-17.
50 Ibid 35.

increase to the kingdom of God of 10,000,000 people in two years!

The fruit of the Revival could never have been reaped if Lanphier gave into discouragement after the first twenty minutes of that initial prayer meeting. No one had shown up! He could have put a sign on the door that said, "Prayer Meeting Cancelled for Today." What if he had given up after having only six people come the first week? What if he had not proved faithful? Through the prayers of what began with six believers, God unleashed His Spirit in a way that affected the entire country.

> "The influence of the Awakening was felt everywhere in the nation. It first captured the great cities, but it also spread through every town and village and country hamlet. It swamped schools and colleges. It affected all classes without respect to condition. A Divine influence seemed to pervade the land, and men's hearts were strangely warmed by a Power that was outpoured in unusual ways."[51]

The heart of one man burdened by the state of affairs in his city invited strangers to join him for noonday prayer. Oh how God honors the bent heart of the human soul.

Prayer and the Revivals of 1904-1906

Like the First Great Awakening the revivals of 1904-1906 began overseas and shortly thereafter ignited a new work of the Holy Spirit in North America. It began when Evan Roberts' burden for the land of Wales moved him to seek the Lord in a way that outpaced his peers. In his mid-twenties, Roberts sought the Lord for personal revival. And after receiving a "baptism of the Holy Spirit" he felt compelled to leave college and return home to speak to the youth of his church. His simple message to the curious congregation of sixteen listeners unleashed a revival that led to at least 70,000 conversions.[52] What was the message God gave to Roberts? 1) Confess all known sin. 2) Deal with and get rid of anything "doubtful" in your life. 3) Be ready to obey the Holy Spirit instantly. 4) Confess Christ publicly.[53]

The message and anointing of this young man was fueled by the prayers of others who preceded him. One source explains, "The true origin of the movement is

---

[51] Ibid 21.
[52] S.B. Shaw, *The Great Revival in Wales* (Pensacola FL: Christian Life Books. 2002) 179.
[53] Ibid 85.

probably to be found in the prayer circles which have honeycombed Wales for the last eighteen months. The people who had banded themselves together were crying out mightily for a revival, and God at length graciously answered the prayers of His saints."[54]

G. Campbell Morgan made the same point when he wrote,

> "a praying remnant has been agonizing before God about the state of the beloved land, and it is through that the answer of fire has come . . . It is a Divine visitation in which God – let me say this reverently – in which God is saying to us; See what I can do without the things you are depending on; see what I can do in answer to a praying people; see what I can do through the simplest, who are ready to fall in line, and depend wholly and absolutely upon Me."[55]

During the years of 1904-05, the revival in Wales was marked, not by preaching, but by a spirit of prayer and repentance pervading churches. While the revival started with Roberts, he avoided being seen as the key figure of the revival. He wanted God's Spirit to be the center of the movement, and God's Spirit worked in church after church in response to the spirit of prayer among God's people.

An account from Charlotte Chapel in Edinburgh, Scotland by Rev. Joseph Kemp describes the spirit of prayer that spread beyond Roberts' homeland.

> "By the end of 1905, the church had been praying one whole year without a break. Night after night, week after week, month after month, the prayer meetings went on increasing in numbers and intensity. It is impossible to convey any adequate idea of the prayer passion that characterized those meetings. There was little or no preaching, it being a common experience for the pastor to go to the pulpit on the Lord's Day and find the congregation so caught in the spirit of prayer as to render preaching out of the question."[56]

When the outbreak of revival occurred in the United Kingdom, a hunger for God grew in North America. The Spirit stirred among a contingent of the Methodist Episcopal Church known as the Holiness Movement, boiling up without a vent for the intensifying spiritual pressure. Unified in opposition to the progressive branch of the Methodist church and the growing influence of Modernism, the Holiness movement promoted camp meetings across the nation during the

---

[54] Ibid 57.

[55] Ibid 117.

[56] Olford 129

post civil war years.[57] As Methodist opposition toward the Holiness Movement hardened, Holiness churches sprang up everywhere. These congregations had an openness to the things being reported to them about the revival in Wales.

This predisposition toward a new work of God led to the Pentecostal outpouring on Azusa Street in Los Angeles. Leaders from Holiness churches had both corresponded[58] with and visited Evan Roberts.[59] They had prayed in earnest for such a blessing in California. Born in the humblest of humble settings, the outpouring of the Holy Spirit on the Azusa Street congregation in Los Angeles set fire to the stacked wood of the Holiness Movement.

Like the First Great Awakening, the revival of 1906 was also associated with a powerful earthquake.[60] The 1906 San Francisco earthquake occurred within a week of the spiritual earthquake on Azusa Street.[61] The combined events stirred believers and Christian leaders from across the country, and they descended upon Azusa Street to receive the baptism of the Holy Spirit and spread the revival to their home communities.

What were the results of the revival? As of the year 2000 the Pentecostal – Charismatic branch of the evangelical church accounted for an estimated 550,000,000 in world-wide membership.[62] It all started because a godly remnant concerned for the state of the world and Church began to pray. As one secular historian observed the phenomenon of America's great moves of revival, he summarized the trend. "The Great Awakenings have not usually originated from the top; generally, they welled up from below and have often been given voice by ministers and novice leaders on the fringes of the establishment."[63]

We should understand that "novice leaders on the fringe of the establishment" are the type of people God puts His hand upon in times of revival. They are the group which cries out for a new work of God in their midst. Their pattern of heart-felt, agonizing, persistent prayer for revival is undeniably connected to the

---

[57] Synan 30-31.
[58] Frank Bartleman, *Azusa Street* (New Kensington, PA: Whitaker House, 1982) 12.
[59] Ibid 31.
[60] The great earthquake of 1727 was the culmination of a number of natural disasters in New England. The earthquake of 1727 was significant enough to stir second and third generation settlers to begin thinking about the role of God in their affairs. An article describing the event can be found on the Website of the USGS (United States Geological Survey). http://earthquake.usgs.gov/regional/states/events/1727_11_10.php
[61] Synan 98.
[62] Synan 281.
[63] Ibid 41

movement which follows.

Prayer and the Greatest Awakening of Them All

We should not be surprised by the pattern of pre-revival prayer since that was the pattern established in the greatest movement of the Holy Spirit ever to break forth: Acts 2. In the days before Pentecost, prayer played a prominent role. As the apostles and disciples waited for Pentecost to arrive, they spent the time giving themselves to prayer. "*These all with one mind were continually devoting themselves to prayer, along with the women, and Mary the mother of Jesus, and with His brothers*" (Acts 1:14).

These early believers demonstrated for us the attitudes and activities that precede the outpouring of the Holy Spirit. They were united "*with one mind.*" Being united in prayer with brothers and sisters in Christ plays an integral part in bringing revival. We saw this with the Holy Club of the 18th century, the businessman's prayer meeting of the 19th century, and the bands of concerned Welshmen in the 20th century. A dramatic new work begins with a portion of God's people *unified* in prayer.

> "A dramatic new work begins with a portion of God's people *unified* in prayer."

The Scripture also says that they were "*constantly devoting themselves to prayer.*" That speaks of their commitment to prayer. Pre-revival praying shows itself as an inescapable burden that gets hold of believers. They seek the Lord with a passion, diligence and fire that will not stop until God answers it. The Apostles could have strategized, organized and evangelized without the Holy Spirit, but until He energized them, their efforts would have been fleshly and weak. In those days between Calvary and Pentecost, the fledgling leadership of the Christian Church wisely devoted themselves to prayer.

Their humility and inclusiveness as they prayed also instructs us. It is not an insignificant detail that, along with the Apostles, others prayed as well: "*the women, and Mary the mother of Jesus, and with His brothers.*" Humility enters the meeting when those other than the twelve are included, especially the fact that this prayer meeting crossed gender lines. Men and women praying together was new. It was not just the Apostles but everyone who desired to seek the Lord who prayed. Mary and Jesus' brothers were also in attendance, significant because at one point during Jesus' ministry His relatives thought He had lost His mind (Mark 3:21)! On another occasion His brothers revealed a high degree of unbelief in Him (John 7:1-5). Having overcome their doubts and concerns, His relatives submitted their hearts to *their* risen Lord too, and attached themselves to the other early disciples. They could not have done so without humility. This humility indicates that they had the courage to make everything in their lives right, clean and pure as they waited in prayer.

We see some of the same elements in Acts 4 where the Holy Spirit gets poured out a second time. In that passage, a number of disciples gathered for prayer in response to the threats of religious opponents. The Bible says, *"They lifted up their voices with one accord"* (Acts 4:24). They sought God at the same time, in the same place with the same mind.

They also prayed *boldly*. They do not pray to be protected from harm or kept from suffering but rather, *"grant that Your bond-servants may speak Your word with all confidence, while You extend Your hand to heal, and signs and wonders take place through the name of Your holy servant Jesus"* (Acts 4:29-30). Rather than praying for a reversal in their circumstances they ask for the confidence to declare the message and for signs to confirm the message! How does God view such united prayer in the face of opposition? *"And when they had prayed, the place where they had gathered together was shaken, and they were all filled with the Holy Spirit and began to speak the word of God with boldness"* (Acts 4:31).

Common Threads

Let me summarize the common threads which run through the biblical examples of pre-revival prayer as well as in the more recent expressions in the great revivals:
1) A small number of concerned individuals gathered for the purpose of prayer.
2) Unity of purpose pervaded their prayers.
3) A passion for God infused their prayers.

Prayer for revival is not a passing fad or brief exercise of the deeper life. It breaks the heart of the petitioners in the process and leads us to cry out like Evan Roberts, "Bend Me!"[64] The cry is not only for oneself, but for one's church, that through God's fresh blessing upon one's congregation, one's community might again feel the life-altering impact of the gospel.

---

[64] Evan Robert's signature heart cry, "Bend Me!" speaks of the brokenness and selflessness revival requires.

Summary

Praying this way may seem daunting. We may feel as if we will never be prepared. Or, we might feel there are too many obstacles to unity in our church for revival praying to be effective. Tozer sums up the challenge when he writes, ". . . we should be encouraged to know that God does not wait for perfection in any church. A smaller group within the larger body may be the key to revival. They who compose this group need only become united in heart and purpose and God will begin a work in them, a work which may go on to embrace larger numbers as they meet the simple conditions. The greater the number in any church who are of one heart and one mind the more powerfully will the Spirit move . . . but He never waits for an every-member participation."[65]

Pre-revival prayer starts as burdened individuals ask God to have His way in them and in their church.

Any volunteers?

---

[65] A.W. Tozer, *Paths to Power* 64.

Chapter Six

If my people ...
will seek my face

"God desires to set up His throne in our hearts and reign there without a rival. In some the revolt is obvious and overt. In others, it is hidden. But in both cases, we have become estranged from our rightful Lord."
- William Wilberforce

"At New Year's 1739, George Whitefield, my brother Charles, three others and I, with about sixty of our brethren, were present at a love feast on Fetter Lane. About three in the morning, as we were continuing in prayer, the power of God came upon us so mightily that many cried out in holy joy, while others were knocked to the ground. As soon as we were recovered a little from the awe and amazement at the presence of God, we broke out in one voice, 'We praise Thee, O God; we acknowledge Thee to be the Lord.'"[66]   John Wesley's record of the outpouring of the Holy Spirit on the leaders of the Evangelical Awakening reminds us of the kind of outpouring we long to see. Can God do it again? We can have hope for a similar outpouring if we seek God's face as intentionally as did the early leaders of Methodism.

In the Scriptures, the idea of intentionally seeking God's face assumes that He has turned His face away from us. Micah 3:4 says, *"Then they will cry out to the Lord but He will not answer them. Instead, He will hide His face from them at that time, because they have practiced evil deeds."* David cries out in Psalm 13:1-2, *"How long, O Lord? Wilt Thou forget me forever? How long wilt Thou*

---

[66] Weakley 77.

hide Thy face from me . . . How long will my enemy be exalted over me?" God uses affliction to motivate us to seek His face when we have sinned: "*I will go away and return to My place until they acknowledge their guilt and seek My face. In their affliction they will earnestly seek Me*" (Hosea 5:15). Seeking God's face requires a measure of responsiveness on our part, "*When Thou didst say, 'Seek My face,' my heart said to Thee, 'Thy face, O Lord, I shall seek'*" (Psalm 27:8).

Seeking the Lord's face includes a plea that His countenance toward us would be transformed, "*Make Thy face to shine upon Thy servant*" (Psalm 31:16). Seeking God's face recognizes that His face turned away from us and we in earnest sincerity seek that it might once again shine favorably upon us.

To regain His favorable disposition toward us, either individually or corporately, we must become aware of those things which caused the lapse in His blessing. Seeking God's face means ascertaining His opinion of our condition. We seek His face in an honest effort to know those things of which we need to repent and of which we are likely unaware. We seek to gain His diagnosis on our corporate and personal spiritual health.

How Does God Speak to a Church?

We must find ways to discern what He is saying to us both corporately and personally. Methods of seeking His face personally are more familiar to us than discerning His voice corporately. When we seek the Lord as individuals, He often speaks through His Word, convicting us with a particular passage that flashes like a neon sign to our souls. He may also use the influence of a courageous friend who confronts our sin. He can use preaching or simply a quiet moment of reflection when we suddenly see what He wants to convey to us.

But if revival is a corporate endeavor, as 2 Chronicles 7:14 suggests, how does God speak to His people *collectively*? The Lord no longer sends individual letters to churches as he did to the seven churches in Revelation 2 and 3. But perhaps those same letters reveal how loudly He speaks to your church without you realizing it.

The Lord based His letters in Revelation on each church's history. The churches received both commendations and condemnations based on the facts of their history up to the point in time of each letter. The question for us is simple: If the Lord of the Church were to take a look at the history of your local church, what would He say to you based on that history? And, to change the focus slightly, what was God saying to your church through the challenges and crises your church faced in its history? Did you listen? These divine messages behind the key events in your church's history are known as "metamessages."

Meta – What?

A metamessage is communication contained in the intentions surrounding an event or a repeated series of events. Metamessages are intended implications drawn from the literal message or pattern of events that unfold. Clear as mud? Let me try to explain with a simple one question quiz for married men: Husbands, which is the correct response to the following reminder from your wife? She says, "Honey, *we* need to take out the trash." Do you respond with:

A) "Ok – *we* can take out the trash together whenever you're ready."
B) "Yes dear. When are *you* free to take out the trash with me?"
C) "Thanks for the reminder honey, *I'll* take care of it."

Any answer other than "C" reflects an inadequate understanding of most communication in marriage! Someone once said, "No man is truly married until he understands every word his wife is *not* saying."

This quiz helps us realize we know what metamessages are, we simply have not formally recognized them as such. Reminding her husband to take out the trash with the statement, "*We* need to take out the trash," she uses what I like to call the "masculine singular form of the plural pronoun 'we.'" The surface message in her reminder is that the trash needs to go out. The metamessage is "You, dear husband, need to take care of it." She is not suggesting a new activity for the two of you on a date night! Rather she gives a message within a message, or a *meta*message.

Metamessages are found in certain behaviors, actions, or words that acquire additional meanings over time. When you're in a social setting, perhaps a fancy restaurant, and your spouse gives you "that LOOK" across the table (you know the LOOK I'm talking about), it doesn't necessarily mean you have something stuck in your teeth. It means whatever it has come to mean over the years in the context of your relationship with each other.

Dr. Kenneth Quick in his class on "Church and Community Exegesis" describes metamessages this way, "A metamessage is a larger, deeper, message found in symbolic or repeated actions and words often going on for a long time."[67] Deborah

---

[67] Dr. Kenneth Quick, (Church and Community Exegesis, Notes) 5

Tannen writes, "The metamessage is information about the relations among the people involved and their attitudes about what they are saying or doing and the people they are saying or doing it to . . . Essentially, metamessages let us know what is going on beyond the words."[68]

Let's take a look at an example from Scripture. John 8:58-59 states, "*Jesus said to them, 'Truly, truly, I say to you, before Abraham was born, I am.' Therefore they picked up stones to throw at Him.*"

First, a little background: The Jews thought Jesus was demon-possessed because He claimed that whoever kept his teaching would never taste death. They wanted to know who He thought He was to make such a claim. They told Him there was no way he was more esteemed than Abraham or the prophets who themselves died. John 8:58-59 represents Jesus' reply to the question: Who do you think you are? The surface message Jesus gave them was, "I am older than Abraham" – "*before Abraham was born I am.*" What was the metamessage? "I am God." Did Jesus come out and say those three words? No. Did the Jews get the metamessage? The Jews knew the last two words of Jesus' statement were code for a claim to divinity. Their subsequent actions, "*Therefore they picked up stones to throw at him,*" were also a metamessage communicating their rejection of Jesus' claim. A metamessage is the message behind or within the actions or communication. When things happen within a church, we should reflect, "***What is God doing or saying through this pattern of events?***"

When the Ephesian church received their letter from the Lord in Revelation 2:2-6, it was written using the second person singular pronoun "you" as were all the other six letters to the churches. Jesus used that particular word in describing both the sins and the affirmations of all the churches. What metamessages did Jesus send in addressing the church as a whole rather than as particular individuals?

> "I know **your** (singular, et al.) deeds, **your** hard work and **your** perseverance. I know that **you** cannot tolerate wicked men, that **you** have tested those who claim to be apostles but are not, and have found them false. **You** have perse-vered and have endured hardships for my name, and have not grown weary. Yet I hold this against **you**: **You** have forsaken **your** first love. Remember the height from which **you** have fallen! Repent and do the things **you** did at first. If **you** do not repent, I will come to **you** and remove **your** lampstand from its

---

[68] Deborah Tannen, *You Just Don't Understand; Women and Men in Conversation* (New York; William Morris & Co. 1990) 32.

place. But *you* have this in *your* favor: *You* hate the practices of the Nicolaitans, which I also hate."[69]

Here are a few of the metamessages I believe we can see. Perhaps you'll identify more on your own.

1) The Ephesian believers got off track *as a church*.
2) They lost their first love *as a church*, not as individuals.
3) Their losses and gains were measured *as one body* not as individuals.
4) An individual is *not exempt* from responsibility for larger issues in the church. One cannot say, "I didn't do it," or "I was not there when that happened."
5) The Lord holds *the entire church* accountable and calls them to repentance as a corporate entity.
6) The Lord will not violate His principles of usability. A church must meet His standards corporately if they hope to enjoy His blessing.

Recognizing that Jesus addressed the Ephesian believers as a corporate whole, we accomplish two things: First, our understanding of metamessages grows; second, we learn that the Lord looks at churches *corporately*—as a single entity—not just as autonomous individuals loosely assembled under one steeple. He holds churches accountable as a whole and calls them to repent corporately as well. He also affirms them corporately. Many Christians in North America find this an alien idea. We largely reflect our culture's individualistic orientation. We carry this "individual mindset" into our pursuit of revival, misunderstanding how it works. All the while the Lord looks at how we function together as His body and holds us accountable for the condition of His Bride. How important then is it to know the history of your church and what the Lord is saying to your corporate body?

> "When God speaks to His people, He often uses pain to do so."

Pain – God's Metamessage of Choice

When God speaks to His people, He often uses pain to do so. The Scriptures demonstrate that pain is God's metamessage of choice. God *arranges painful events* among His people to bring them back to Himself. The things we must discern are: 1) is this pain we are going through a metamessage from God? And

---

[69] Kenneth Quick, *Healing the Heart of Your Church* (St. Charles, IL: ChurchSmart 2003) 22.

2) what is He trying to show us about ourselves through painful events and, more importantly, through a *pattern* of similar painful events?

Whatever that issue is which God has with us, it stands between us and His blessing. Seeking His face means coming to understand where we have gone off track, and its goal is righting whatever He shows us. God inflicts pain on us in order to alert us to the problem. The pain itself—and where it is located—often exposes the underlying problem He wants us to address.[70] The Bible is full of examples where God used corporate pain to alert His people to their sin.

For instance, after the death of Joshua, the people of Israel began to compromise with the cultures around them, assimilating idolatry into their corporate lifestyle. The summary statement of their regression is found in Judges 2:13-14, *"So they forsook the Lord and served Baal and the Asherah. And the anger of the Lord burned against Israel, and He gave them into the hands of the plunderers who plundered them; and He sold them into the hands of the their enemies around them, so that they could no longer stand before their enemies."* Forsaking the Lord, the Israelite community came under painful pressures inflicted by God. They faced economic devastation through plundering; they lost their freedom as they were given over to their enemies; they had no strength to face the forces that dominated them. We might see that situation and think they had a political problem or an economic problem or even a national security problem. Drawing such conclusions falls short of an accurate diagnosis of their plight.

Their troubles were symptoms of a deeper problem to which God drew their attention: they *"forsook the Lord."* The painful crises were God's metamessage that something was very wrong. However, their pain was not the main issue; it rather pointed them to a deeper, more significant problem. The *type* of pain they faced was a clue to the deeper problem. They were sold into the hands of enemies who worshipped the foreign gods to which they had sold themselves. God used an idolatrous people to dominate Israel as a metamessage indicating Israel's root sin of idolatry. If only they had had eyes to see and ears to hear!

In Haggai's day, God's people did not overtly forsake the Lord. Rather they became indifferent and preoccupied with their own comforts. As they went about their day to day lives they ignored the destitute condition of the temple. What does God do to get their attention? He institutes a cycle of diminishing returns on their normally productive economy: *"You have sown much, but harvest little;*

---

[70] From conversations with Dr. Ken Quick during the development of supplemental materials for *Healing the Heart of Your Church*.

you eat, but there is not enough to be satisfied; you drink, but there is not enough to become drunk; you put on clothing, but no one is warm enough; and he who earns, earns wages to put into a purse with holes. Thus says the Lord of hosts, Consider your ways!" (Haggai 1:6)

Can you imagine the Israelites' frustration? They experienced a "one step forward, two steps back" lifestyle. God used want, lack, and loss to get them to consider their ways. Was this a "purse problem" since the Lord says, *"He who earns, earns wages to put into a purse with holes?"* Did they have a clothing problem since no one was warm enough? Human ingenuity might have led them to knit more sweaters or invent more secure handbags!

They looked at all these dilemmas as part of their *normal routine*, as problems to overcome. They did not see divine discipline for what it was until the pain became too much to bear. Their root problems were not economic or agricultural; they were spiritual. The Lord urged them through the prophet, *"Consider your ways!"* Their personal impoverishment pointed to the impoverishment of the temple. God used pain to speak to them, and the kind of pain He sent reflected the issue that offended Him.

Can you tell me where the following text is found in the Bible: *"If I shut up the heavens so that there is no rain, or if I command the locust to devour the land or if I send pestilence among my people . . . "*? Here is the next verse: *"If my people who are called by my name will humble themselves and pray and seek my face and turn from their wicked ways, then will I forgive their sin and heal their land."* God sends varied forms of pain among His people. Why? So we will humble ourselves and pray and seek His face. He knows that we will not humble ourselves otherwise!

Here is the kicker: God uses that pain to lead us to revival if we listen to its message! Corporate pain is God's metamessage that something is seriously wrong among His people, whether in the church or in the nation. Without Divine pressure being applied we might go on plugging the holes in our declining economy, propping up our eroding morality, or revamping our broken political system. These problems act as God's hammer to break us and bring us to our knees, stirring us to seek His face. God uses pain to prepare us for His blessing . . . if we listen.

God applies the lashes of pain very specifically. In Amos 4, the prophet describes the various targeted manifestations of divine discipline God sent among His people. And yet, sadly, they did not respond to Him. *"And furthermore, I withheld rain from you while there were still three months until harvest. Then I would send rain on one city and on another city I would not send rain. One part would be rained on while the other part not rained on would dry up. So two or three cities would stagger to another city to drink water, but would not be satisfied. Yet you have not returned to Me . . .*" (4:7, 8). God focuses pain on specific places at specific times to get specific peoples' attention. Are we hearing the metamessages He sends to us through pain?

This approach to discern what the Lord says through pain may have been forgotten but its biblical reality cannot be denied. The early European settlers of this continent understood it. They called for days of fasting and prayer in light of crises or disasters (corporate pain). Here is an excerpt from a proclamation issued by the Council of the Massachusetts Bay Colony held in Boston on March 10th, 1668;

> "The Governour and Magistrates being assembled in Council and in some measure sensible of the many tokens of the Lord's displeasure against us, the cutting short the fruits of the earth sundry years past and otherwise bringing us low more than formerly, together with the many provoking evils that do abound among us to the great dishonor of God and our profession of His holy name . . . Do therefore commend to all the inhabitants of this colony the twenty fifth day of this instant to be kept a Public Day of Humiliation and spent in fasting and prayer to the Lord for pardon of whatever have been or are provoking to His holy eyes, and that He will be pleased to give unto us, from the greatest to the least, truly to repent of all our sins . . . *that* His blessing upon our present seed-time *may return*; that so it may appear that the Lord's anger is turned away from us . . . Also the present low estate of the churches of Christ in Europe, and especially in our own dear Native Country is to be humbly presented before the Lord." (Italics mine)
>
> By the Council,
> Edward Rawson, Secretary.[71]

Vestiges of such powers granted to civil authorities—calling us to fasting and prayer—can still be found in modern legislative documents. The Governor of Georgia for example has the legal right to call for days of special fasting and prayer. "The 1984 General Assembly changed state law with respect to public and legal holidays observed in Georgia. The new law (O.C.G.A. sec. 1-4-1) provides:

> (a) The State of Georgia shall recognize and observe as public and legal holidays:

---

[71] *Sanctify the Congregation*, Appendix C p335

(1) All days which have been designated as of January 1, 1984, as public and legal holidays by the federal government; and (2) All other days designated and proclaimed by the Governor as public and legal holidays or as days of *fasting and prayer* or other religious observance."[72] (Italics mine).

Imagine the circumstances under which a modern-day governor might feel compelled to call for such a response. Doing so would mean pain had overtaken the State in the form of drought, war, famine or an economic crisis. Under normal circumstances, a day of fasting and prayer appears unwarranted to us. Without great pain to motivate people to seek His face, it's unlikely such an occasion would ever be called.

Pain in the History of a Church

We have seen how God used corporate pain in Israel. But how does the principle of corporate pain relate to God's people on a local church level?

God uses pain in our local congregations just as He did in Israel. The kinds of pain may change but the principle remains the same: crises in the history of a local church are indicators of a deeper problem just as war, oppression and drought were in Israel. Until we understand the meaning of our corporate pain and its repetitive nature, our progress toward revival will be limited in our church. Our pre-revival confession and repentance will be too shallow to be effective.

Recurring Corporate Pain

The church is described as the "Body of Christ" in the New Testament, and, just as in the human body, pain serves a crucial function in the Body of Christ. It lets us know our church body has a disease, an injury, or unseen malfunction. What is God trying to tell us through our corporate pain? A painful crisis or series of crises in a church is God telling your church something is seriously amiss. The pain continues because you have not learned the lesson and the pain intensifies until you are finally ready to visit the Great Physician.

Quick makes this comment: "God keeps taking His people around and around through similar experiences until they finally learn the lessons that allow them to make further progress. Could that explain our church's problems in the present? Are they taking yet another trip around Mt. Sinai?"[73] The chronic pain in our

---

[72] Georgia.gov <http://www.georgia.gov/00/article/0,2086,4802_64437763_67467812,00.html>
[73] Quick 23.

corporate histories can come in the form of church splits, moral failures, reactive conflicts, pastoral or congregational abuse, financial crisis or unresolved shame. All are examples of ways in which the Lord speaks loudly to us of His displeasure, just as in Israel. He wants us to recognize the root problem that allows these difficulties to occur in the first place. If we refuse to get the message through our corporate pain, God may prearrange for us to go through similar circumstances until we get the message. Figure 6.1 demonstrates how one traumatic crisis can follow another until we figure them out.

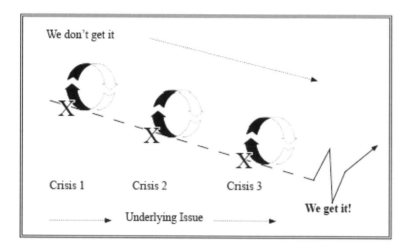

Figure 6.1

We tend to see each trauma in our church's history as an individual event and not understand its relationship to the others. We fail to recognize them as metamessages from God to our congregation. We know that we have ugly spats from time to time or painful splits. The lay leadership and the pastor find themselves in repeated upheavals. The choir director takes off with a deacon; the treasurer takes off with the money. Take your pick. Define the crisis with whatever sad events you like. We see painful crises as something that must be endured, ignored or deplored. We have not realized that there may be a connection between the crises. We see them as individual unrelated painful events. All the while our spiritual energies get sapped and the culture of our church gets shaped by the residual effects of the ugly, painful mess.

If God speaks to us through the repetition of pain, indicating a deeper problem, we must ask God for discernment. Was there a point in time when the church's ministry went from fruitful to frustrating? That was the point at which God found something He did not like in your church. You will make no significant, pain-free progress until the issue gets addressed. The path of revival is blocked.

Corporate pain can result from a crisis in any one of the three areas Jesus addressed in the history of the seven churches. It can manifest itself through a church's deeds, devotion or doctrine. A church can suffer a slow painful death as the result of diminishing devotion for the Lord and love for each other.

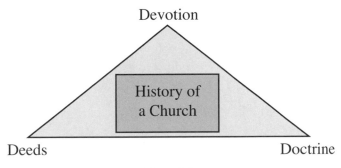

Figure 6.2

Departure from orthodox doctrine also impedes God's blessing and leaves more than its share of wounds in local churches and denominations. It can be conflict over core doctrines like the authority of Scripture, and also conflict over secondary issues that grieve the Holy Spirit. But the largest category of corporate offense is deeds and conduct. Various forms of bad behavior in the corporate setting mar our churches as not measuring up before the Lord.

These crises are not always what they seem. When conflict or pain enters the body of Christ, it should stir us to cry out: "Lord, why have you allowed this pain to enter our body? What are You trying to show us about ourselves through these events? Lord, what's the real issue here?"

This is not a passing inquiry but involves a commitment to review your church's history to observe any pattern of pain that may exist. When did the pain first start? Was there a split that led to the formation of a new church? Was there a conflict over worship styles? Perhaps a passive board never confronted a sin or took a daring step of faith it should have. Maybe your church chewed up its pastors or its pastors chewed up its boards. Perhaps shameful events went uncorrected or destructive mavericks wounded the body. Maybe you've had a destructive annual church meeting, or two or three. Do you view these things as *normal*? Is it any wonder that revival bypasses existing churches manifesting such pitiful behavior? If we test the Lord enough, He may place us in a wilderness until that generation of transgressors passes away, or we come to our senses and seek His face.

A large portion of local churches sit wounded and dysfunctional because they choose to gloss over their history and fail to see God's hand in their pain. Churches like this live in a world of their own making. Because they do not deal biblically with conflict, *painful* events go ignored in the corporate psyche. Olson says, "Dysfunctional churches often have buried stories that never surface."[74] Until these stories are revisited and addressed, revival, re-blessing and meaningful ministry will all seem like a distant dream – no matter what your ministry model. Until the painful episodes of your corporate history are attended to in the way God requires, the "fellowship" you experience has little resemblance to the fellowship you were designed to enjoy. Rather, a false form of fellowship governs your relationships; they become shallow, limited to greetings and small-talk on Sunday morning. Church folk who meet together in an unhealthy environment may do so for years without *really* knowing each other.

The health of local churches determines the health of the Church and the health of the Church is the only hope for the health of our nation. Conversely, the ill-health of our nation reflects the ill health of the Church and its local expressions. We cannot continue to ignore the unresolved wounds and destructive sin in our local churches because God does not. It is ludicrous to imagine He will revive a church where unresolved wounds and historical sin abide. If He does send revival, He will raise up new movements outside the diseased congregations, leaving them to continue in decline. But if unhealthy churches across this land begin to seek His face and discern what the Lord is saying through their corporate pain, then there is the hope for new blessing and renewed corporate health.[75]

A Case Study in Point

The events described in the following case study come from the history of a nine year-old church in Douglasville, Georgia. It was my privilege to be with them as they wrestled with forces that locked them in a cycle of recurring pain. Together we journeyed through the church's history and sought to discern what God was saying through it.

Local Culture

My first Sunday there I found their worship inspiring. Whatever problems this small group of believers had, the presence of the Lord still met with them in

---

[74] Olson 135.

[75] If you are serious about considering the role corporate pain plays in the history of your church, I refer you to, *Healing the Heart of Your Church*, by Dr. Kenneth Quick. You can also visit Blessing Point Ministries – www.blessingpoint.org.

worship. After the service, my wife and I went out for lunch with two couples from the church. That's when I began to gain insight into the local culture and understand the church's problems. I chatted with Robert, a member of the church's leadership team, and asked him how he would describe the culture of Douglasville. He told me of a community largely marked by rebellion. Rebellion went back to the very founding of the county.

Douglas County was formed in 1870 out of parts of two neighboring counties. To gain support for the new entity, local leaders petitioned the state legislature – which was dominated by Republican, Reconstructionists. To gain the legislators' favor, local leaders proposed naming the county after Fredrick Douglass. Douglass was a former slave and abolitionist before the Civil War and a Republican leader after the Civil War. Incorporation was approved. However in the mid 1870's when Democrats controlled county government, most of whom were confederate veterans, a local official dropped one "s" from the county name. The honored namesake of the county was now Stephen A. Douglas the senator who ran against Abraham Lincoln in the 1860 presidential election![76]

The same spirit of rebellion, I came to learn, also infected the larger Christian community. Many of the churches in the county were a result of other churches splitting. It was suggested that church growth in Douglas County was often a matter of disgruntled believers migrating from one church to another.

Church Background

Emmanuel Fellowship itself started from a split with a larger congregation in Douglasville. The split appeared passive rather than openly aggressive in nature. It was described as "people independently but simultaneously deciding to leave a church that condoned unethical behavior by the senior pastor." The week after the exodus, phone calls passed back and forth to find out what each of the departed was going to do. As a result, they decided to meet together. The church began with about 125 people.

They brought on a pastor who, after a short ministry with them, departed under heated circumstances. This caused a *second* church split! They had gone through two pastors in that short time and then their third pastor came on board.

About a year before their third pastor's departure there was a third upheaval.

[76] See: http://www.rootsweb.ancestry.com/~gadougla/douglas_county_by_joe_baggett.htm
http://www.experiencefestival.com/a/Douglas_County_Georgia_-_History/id/4994793
http://en.wikipedia.org/wiki/Douglas_County,_Georgia

Again the church split, leaving this pastor looking for a new ministry and the twenty to thirty attendees which remained suffering from bewilderment and fatigue.

The Process

After filling in for a few weeks, the subject came up of my becoming their interim pastor. I consented to serve as their interim but attached a condition: that we review the church's history to determine what God might be saying to us.[77]

We scheduled three nights in a row during September 2004 to discuss these issues. One leader, Mike, had health problems and could not attend until later in the process. Although disappointing at first, we later saw God's purpose in this. Each meeting lasted from 7 pm to 10 pm, sometimes later. The following is a break down of our discussions as they unfolded.

Night One

Through the course of that first night we listed clues as to what we thought God was trying to tell us. These clues consisted of both observations and symptoms the leadership saw as they looked at the church. We wrote down ideas on sheets of flip chart paper, posting them around the room. Authority issues quickly became a focus. There were unclear ideas about who held authority in the church and there seemed to be a problem with authority itself.

Curiously, we noted that the church had an identity problem. Someone described it as a "church that did not want to be a church." (I jokingly commented, "Maybe we needed to find them a pastor who did not want to be a pastor!") Moreover, the congregation resisted any kind of change. Disunity and stubbornness characterized the church leadership. They ignored problems until they became volcanic. And, perhaps most compelling of all, the church as a body had developed a culture that felt okay with amputation to solve its conflicts. They had grown to accept church splits as normative.

We looked at these symptoms and saw them to be rooted in previous betrayal by authority figures, which resulted in an unwillingness to trust them anymore. However, in making that observation, we still didn't feel we had reached the heart of the matter for Emmanuel Fellowship.

---

[77] The process of doing a historical review is spelled out in *Healing the Heart of Your Church*, by Dr. Kenneth Quick. A Facilitator's Guide and Participant's Workbook are also available at ChurchSmart Resources (www.churchsmart.com).

The lay leaders were frank: They came with no axes to grind, sincerely interested in restoring the well-being of their church. Those of you who work with church leaders can appreciate the courage these men showed. The Lord appreciated their efforts too because, as we closed in prayer that night, the Holy Spirit filled the room. When we said the last "amen," no one wanted to move. It was one of those holy moments when you don't know what to do next and conversation seems awkward. In retrospect, our experience in prayer encouraged us to return for a second, even more painful night.

Night Two

Our goal the second night was to construct a chart that reflected the church's entire history. It covered the good things that had come their way, the various locations in which they met, the pastors they had, their attendance over the nine years, and the major crises they faced. I learned more about that church in one night than most pastors learn about their church in five years. Once we laid out the timeline, certain patterns became clear.

First, the church had experienced three heart-rending splits in nine years. Each split, while unique, focused around a male authority figure – the pastor. The split from the original church had been precipitated by the pastor's moral failure and his rejection of discipline. The second split also focused on a pastor. The lay leadership found fault with the pastor's use of time. That pastor departed, and the church, which had been on a bit of a growth trend, lost one third of the congregation. The third and most recent split occurred over the selection of the church's lay leadership team. This was a special case where the pastor possessed legitimate authority to select these men. The church was in a state of redevelopment and the denomination had a strong role in selecting the church's governance through the pastor. However, some of those who were not selected thought they should have been and took issue with the selection process. A growing unwillingness to follow the pastor led to a power struggle and resulted in the most recent split.

A second pattern then presented itself: in spite of the strife that followed this congregation, God sent an occasional significant blessing. Early in their existence they got an opportunity to purchase five acres at a bargain price, which they did in short order. They also grew under the first pastor's ministry. Also, under the last pastor, there was a meaningful baptismal service, a powerful ladies' retreat and God healed one of their leaders of cancer. God showed us that, in spite of the strife, He had a future for them.

Digging deeper into the history of the original split, we wrestled with the spiritual significance of constituted authority. The appointed authority, the man who oversaw the church's response to the fallen pastor in the church from which Emmanuel Fellowship split, decided to handle the situation in a way that some elders did not find agreeable. On that basis they left the church. They thought they were doing the right thing.

At one point I asked a question that touched a nerve, "Do you believe that we are called to submit to spiritual authority even if we believe that the authority figure is wrong?" That triggered a deep discussion about the nature of spiritual authority and their lack of submission in the original split. They grew to realize that the original split was based on rebellion, and that was gut-wrenching. Most saw that the reasons for the original split were not substantive enough to justify it. They realized something else: if the leaders of the original split had not submitted to God's constituted spiritual authority, then by extension they had not submitted to God either. If this were true, they started Emmanuel Fellowship for the wrong reasons. It explained why God had not fully blessed their endeavor.

By the end of that second evening we all left the meeting in excruciating pain. We now saw that the church from its very birth had a problem with submission to authority. The church was born in strife and strife had followed it through its nine-year existence. Upon returning home, I told my wife that I'd be shocked if anyone showed up for the third evening.

Night Three
These were courageous men though, and they did come. As we began our third evening a heavy spirit filled the room. Some uncertainty grew regarding the conclusions we came to the night before. A dear, gifted leader named Phil had been at the church since its founding and he agonized over the implications of the church's beginning. Had the things we talked about the previous evening led us to the right prognosis? Perhaps that first split was justified.

On this night though, I did not have to do any convincing. The majority of the leaders saw things for what they were, and they did the work of bringing those disagreeing in line with what God revealed. The most significant moment of the night occurred when Robert, a retired military man who happens to be African-American, read 1 Peter 2:13-18:

> "Submit yourselves for the Lord's sake to every human institution, whether to a king as the one in authority, or to governors as sent by him for the punishment of evildoers and the praise of those who do right. For such is the will of God that by doing right you may silence the ignorance of foolish men. Act

as free men, and do not use your freedom as a covering for evil, but use it as bond slaves of God. Honor all men; love the brotherhood, fear God, honor the king. ***Slaves be submissive to your masters with all respect, not only to those who are good and gentle, but also to those who are unreasonable.***"

There is something about a Black Christian man reading a passage about slaves submitting to their masters, even to those who are unreasonable, that humbled every Caucasian Christian man in the room. What more could be said? Robert knew what he was reading; he understood the significance of constituted authority from his years in the military. He was God's exclamation point on the pattern of non-submission the Holy Spirit had revealed to us.

That night we got to the heart of the matter with the church. Everyone submitted to the conclusion, and we were of one mind. We went on to discuss questions like: what issues from these conflicts stood unresolved before God? What required repentance and reconciliation toward the other parties involved? We felt we needed to add a fourth night to our meetings in order to plan how we must rectify the situation before God. As we closed in prayer that night and acknowledged our sin as congregational leaders, I sensed God lifting a barrier, a limit; He had placed on the church.

Night Four
On the fourth evening a sense of freedom existed after the previous night's prayer, and I thought our confession had perhaps satisfied the Lord and we did not need to do anything else. Other opinions prevailed. We discussed sending a letter of apology to the man whose authority the leaders of Emmanuel Fellowship had challenged in order to split nine years prior. Some wondered if we could locate him. We decided that, while God might not require it, we wanted to go the extra mile and write an apology to the denominational district office that appointed him.

As we reflected on Emmanuel's second split, it came out that, a few years after leaving, Emmanuel Fellowship's first pastor had written to the church and acknowledged his overreaction at the time of his departure, seeking forgiveness. The existence of this letter was news to most of the men and, sadly the church never responded to it. We felt we now owed him a repentant response, and one individual crafted a reply for the group to sign.

As we considered the circumstances under which their last pastor left, we decided that we required no further action. He had departed some time after the third split and, since the people who remained had great affection for him, he felt blessed as he went to his next ministry.

We determined that the letters alone were not enough. The men also decided that they wanted some symbolic act that demonstrated they were breaking with the sins of the past. They scheduled a meeting the following Sunday night. We would go "on the record" with an official board meeting and then spend time in repentance as leaders of Emmanuel.

Our final action was to plan a Corporate Renewal Service. This special service would allow each of us to share the history of the church and explain the things the Lord had shown us. Then we'd open it up for a corporate time of prayer.

The Confirmations

Mike, the member of the leadership team who was sick during the four nights we met, delivered our first confirmation that our marathon meetings were of God. We explained to him what we discovered, the corrective action we took and would be taking. If Mike had concerns, then it would cast serious doubts about what we thought we had discerned God was saying.

It was clear to Mike that we were on target. He had been at Emmanuel Fellowship almost since the beginning, and he quickly understood the heart of the matter and confirmed that what God had shown us made perfect sense to him.

The second compelling confirmation came as my wife Jeannie and I attended Jeannie's college reunion the week before our planned Corporate Renewal Service. It turned out in God's providence that Emmanuel Fellowship's previous pastor served in a church eight miles from her alma mater. I let him know I would be in town and asked if we could get together. We met and I explained to him all that the church had been through in the last weeks.

When I laid out the story, he and his wife were astounded that the Lord touched the issue they knew had to be addressed. They confirmed what the Holy Spirit revealed about the heart of the matter. They felt that they were not the ones to address those issues, but rejoiced at what the Lord had done to reveal them.

Our third confirmation was the Corporate Renewal Service itself. As each man did his part in the service, it was obvious to me that the leaders really understood and it was no mere intellectual exercise. They internalized the truths we learned and expressed sincere apologies on behalf of previous leadership for what had happened. When we opened it up for corporate prayer, I can only describe it as the closest thing to revival I've experienced. People sincerely repented. The worship team could barely sing. Tears flowed and people got choked up as they confessed their own un-submissive spirits. Some confessions came from people who were hearing for the first time what the leadership had experienced.

We were concerned because visitors were present, but we later learned that these same visitors were touched by the honesty displayed. The Lord used it in their lives. We all left church that day drained but with great expectations of what the Lord was going to do. The repentance service reinvigorated our hopes that God would soon reveal His purpose for Emmanuel Fellowship.

> "Remember, an unresolved issue in your church's past does not mean it is history to God."

Aftermath

Emmanuel Fellowship continues to this day as Hope Community Church. They changed their name in a further effort to break with the patterns of the past. Some of the leaders who went through the historical review process have left now. As the church entered its new era, it did not experience astronomical growth, but it did begin to experience something missing in its experience prior to its re-blessing – conversions! The church gained a level of health and started an outreach that has made it a small but vibrant multicultural ministry. God brought them to the place of new life and corporate revival. He set them free from their cycles of corporate pain as they responded to what He said to them through their history.[78]

Seeking God's Face - Summary

Seeking God's face must not be done superficially. God may have brought your church through painful situations to show you why you must repent. The nature of your crises reflect the underlying problems, just as Emmanuel's repeated church splits pointed to a deeper problem related to authority. They came to see that the various pastoral conflicts they suffered were the symptoms that pointed to the root issue the church needed to face.

Remember, an unresolved issue in your church's past does not mean it is history to God. He brings us through corporate pain to let us know His issues against us. We seek His face to gain His perfect opinion on our condition. We need to hear

---

[78] See Appendix for how God uses recurring cycles of pain in the life of an individual and its relationship to the local church.

from Him about issues of which we may now be blissfully ignorant. If we are courageous enough, God will reveal what we ask him to reveal. The question is: will we seek Him?

Chapter Seven

If my people will turn from their wicked ways

"Every deep revival among God's people must have its roots in a deep sense and confession of sin. Until those who would lead the church in the path of revival bear faithful testimony against the sins of the church, people will be found unprepared."
- Andrew Murray

The *New York Times*, March 20th, 1858, reported the following: "In this city we have beheld a sight which not the most enthusiastic fanatic for church observance could ever have hoped to look upon. We have seen in the business quarters of the city during their busiest hours assemblies of merchants, clerks and working men to the number of five thousand gathering day after day for a simple solemn worship. Similar assemblies we find in other portions of the city, a theatre is turned into a chapel, churches of all sects are open and crowded by day and by night."[79]

When revival catches the attention of a newspaper like the *New York Times* you know something big is in the works. The article cited above describes the scope of a revival New York was experiencing, which subsequently swept across the entire country. Can we, will we see revival on such a grand scale again? The Lord only knows. Yet we might see corporate repentance, healing and revival in the local church——if we face our corporate sin and turn from our wicked ways. The sensational aspects of revival get the attention of the *New York Times*

---

[79] Transcribed from the Heart Cry for Revival Conference 2008 a seminar by John Avant "The Third Great Awakening."

but authentic repentance always makes the headlines in heaven. Jesus said, "*In the same way, I tell you, there is joy in the presence of the angels of God over one sinner who repents*" (Luke 15:10). How much more excitement and joy might there be in heaven when an entire church repents of its hindering sins and responds afresh to the love of God?

God longs for His chosen ones to walk in His love. When we give sin a point of entry into our churches and ignore that sin, He uses pain to alert us to the problem. The motivating force behind providential pain though is an unchanging love. We need only remember the restoration of Peter in the face of three denials or the restoration of Elijah in the face of cowardice to know that any wayward individual or wayward church is not beyond the scope of God's love.

> "How does a church repent?"

The metaphor the Bible uses to describe the Church—"bride"—speaks of affection, commitment and beauty. It reveals the underlying nature of the relationship between Christ and the Church. Of His bride, the Lord says He longs "*to present her to himself as a radiant church, without stain or wrinkle or any other blemish, but holy and blameless*" (Eph. 5:26-27). How does the Bride's appearance relate to corporate repentance? Corporate repentance is the stain remover, the wrinkle releaser, the blemish eraser. Corporate repentance is the Bride's radiance restorer!

The Church's radiance gets renewed by identifying and turning from those things which have tarnished her in the first place. If we teach individual believers to keep short accounts with God through confession and repentance, should we not also prescribe the same principle for the local church? How's your church's radiance level? Do you sense your church is all the Lord intends it to be? Are there unresolved issues in the history of your church which limit God's blessing? The Lord loves the Bride too much to allow her to make significant ministry progress until she addresses the problems before Him.

There are two aspects of repentance we must explore. First is the *nature of repentance* in general. This will be largely familiar to the reader, but it reminds us that repentance, corporate or otherwise, must be authentic to be effective. Second is the *nature of corporate repentance* in specifics. How does a church repent? When Jesus wrote to the Laodiceans in Revelation 3:19 saying, "*Those whom I love, I reprove and discipline; be zealous therefore, and repent,*" He spoke to the *church*. Therefore we must learn how the Lord's command may be satisfied by a local church.

The Nature of Repentance

When 2 Chronicles 7:14 says, *"If my people . . . will . . . turn from their wicked ways"* it suggests two things. First, there were wicked ways from which God's people needed to turn. And second, doing so is the requirement for being "healed," i.e: revival. Through prayer and seeking the Lord, we come face to face with ourselves as God sees us. This reveals behaviors and habits which we have overlooked, self-justified, or did not consider problematic to our spiritual health. Now, however, in the light of the Holy Spirit's illumination, those things we tolerated become the very "ways" from which we must turn.

Voluntarily turning from one's wicked ways involves a *changing of one's mind* about the gravity of the behavior before God. This is what the word repentance means.[80] King David provides a biblical example in Psalm 51. He wrote this psalm after his confrontation with the prophet Nathan, after his confession of adultery and murder. In Psalm 51 we find four key observations associated with a changed mind and turning from one's wicked ways:

1. Turning begins with accepting ownership of and bearing responsibility for our sin:

> [1] Have mercy on *me*, O God,
> according to your unfailing love;
> according to your great compassion
> blot out *my* transgressions.
> [2] Wash away all *my* iniquity
> and cleanse *me* from *my* sin.
> [3] For I know *my* transgressions,
> and *my* sin is always before *me*.
> [4] Against you, you only, have *I* sinned
> and done what is evil in your sight,
> so that you are proved right when you
> speak and justified when you judge.

David's plea for cleansing hinged on God's unfailing love and mercy. Trust in that love enabled him, as it does us, to find the courage to confess how we have failed the Lord. Would we ask God to blot out our transgressions unless we sensed that God's mercy would prevail? David expresses hope in the words, *"Have mercy on me O God, according to your unfailing love, according to your*

---

[80] Bauer 512.

great compassion, blot out my transgressions." Those words are the basis upon which any sinner can approach the throne of grace with the latest mess he or she has made.

Moreover, unfailing love and compassion helped David accept ownership of and take full responsibility for his mess, and it was a big one. David uses the personal pronoun often in this section. He writes of, "*my transgressions*," "*my iniquity*," "*my sin*" and he tells God he has done, "*evil in your sight*." He grasps the guilt caused by his sin and the gravity of what he has done. His offense against God is so deep that, while he has sinned against Bathsheba, against Uriah and against the nation, he can still write, "*Against you, you only have I sinned and done what was evil in your sight.*" He is broken over the matter and how it has affected his relationship with God.

2. Turning involves a deep longing for cleansing from our sin:

> [5] Surely I was sinful at birth and sinful from the
> time my mother conceived me.
> [6] Surely you desire truth in the inner parts;
> you teach me wisdom in the inmost place.
> [7] **Cleanse me** with hyssop, and I will be clean;
> **wash me**, and I will be whiter than snow.
> [8] Let me hear joy and gladness;
> let the bones you have crushed rejoice.
> [9] **Hide** your face from my sins
> and **blot out** all my iniquity.
> [10] **Create in me a pure heart**, O God,
> and **renew** a steadfast spirit within me.

David recognized his intrinsic sinfulness in verse five, "*I was sinful at birth and sinful from the time my mother conceived me.*" He acknowledged that God's standard was inward as well as outward in verse six, "*Surely you desire truth in the inner parts . . . wisdom in the innermost places.*" God required internal authenticity, not merely the outward keeping of the commandments. David's sin left him desperate for God's help and cleansing.

He pleads for cleansing. At least six different allusions to cleansing can be found in verses 7-10. He uses words like cleansing, washing, hiding, blotting out, purifying, and renewing. This quick succession of terms shows us the depth of his guilt. He desperately desires God's cleansing and knows that he cannot cleanse himself.

3. Turning means wrestling with the implications of our sin:

> [11] Do not cast me from your presence
> or take your Holy Spirit from me.
> [12] Restore to me the joy of your salvation
> and grant me a willing spirit, to sustain me.

> [18] In your good pleasure make Zion prosper;
> build up the walls of Jerusalem.
> [19] Then there will be righteous sacrifices,
> whole burnt offerings to delight you;
> then bulls will be offered on your altar.

Truly repentant individuals know they must face how their sin impacted others. We see in verses 11-12 that David knew his sin impacted his relationship with God. He feared a change in his relationship with God, concerned that he had spoiled it entirely. He suddenly grasps what his sin may have cost him. He pleads that the blessings of His relationship with God might not be compromised, *"Do not cast me from your presence or take your Holy Spirit from me."* Who, after gravely sinning, has not inwardly feared the same?

The brief fling with his neighbor's wife cost David dearly. Not only did he jeopardize his relationship with God, but in the last two verses of the Psalm David seems to grasp how his sin may impact the nation. With his plea to *"make Zion prosper,"* David imagines his sin may in some way lead to impoverishment of the nation. It may also affect the city's ability to defend itself, considering his plea to *"build up the walls of Jerusalem."* He did not want his sin to impact the nation he led, but realized it might. The corporate body will often feel the harm when someone in a leadership role sins.

The Bible teaches that God holds the body responsible for the sin of one of its parts. He held the nation of Israel accountable for the sin of a king or a tribe. This was David's fear. David knew he brought trouble on the entire nation and pleads with God to show mercy to the nation despite his sin.

If we have sinned in a way that impacts the body of Christ, our sins damage the corporate whole as David's did. God told him the sword would not depart from his family. That included Absalom's destructive rebellion which tore the fabric of the nation apart. We also must grasp how our sins can infect the Body of Christ and cause it harm. Authentic turning comes to terms with the responsibility we carry for the damage done to others by our sin.

4. Turning includes meaningful symbolic acts that communicate a break with our sin:

> [13] Then *I will teach transgressors your ways*,
> and sinners will turn back to you.
> [14] Save me from bloodguilt, O God,
> the God who saves me,
> and *my tongue will sing of your righteousness*.
> [15] O Lord, open my lips,
> and *my mouth will declare your praise*.
> [16] You do not delight in sacrifice, or I would bring
> it; you do not take pleasure in burnt offerings.
> [17] The sacrifices of God are a broken spirit;
> a broken and contrite heart,
> O God, you will not despise.

In this section of the psalm, David differentiates between meaningful and superficial acts of repentance. He knew what he needed to do to demonstrate authentic turning from sin. He declared sacrifices and burnt offerings superficial in the effort to free himself from the stigma of sin. They were too easy. The repentance in which God delights consists of a contrite heart and a broken spirit—the internal grief over sin validates authentic repentance. It is not enough to go through the motions of repentance or even to break from the offensive behavior. Only when we grasp the destruction sin causes will we flee from its grasp in the future. To simply say we will not do it again or to go through the external measures associated with getting right with God will not suffice. God desires inward adjustments and outward evidence when we deal with our failures.

David declared his desire to bring forth fruits of his repentance. He says he will "*teach transgressors your ways*" and his tongue and mouth will "*sing/declare your praises*." More than rejoicing over being forgiven, this adds public acknowledgment of his sin and of what God did for him. He forsook the secrecy associated with his sin. He doesn't embark on a public relations campaign to restore faith in his leadership. He doesn't outlaw roof top bathing either. Rather he faces his actions squarely, publicly, in a way that helps others learn from his pain and error.

David also highlights God's mercy in his praise for the forgiveness he knows he did not deserve. In doing so he offers hope to all sinners. We need not allow our failure to be our complete undoing. The restoration of David shows that we too can be restored, no matter what we've done.

When we consider what is required in turning from our wicked ways, we begin to realize that only God can lead us to a truly repentant heart. He must help us to thoroughly turn. Our fallen, sinful heart will not discipline itself. We need God to facilitate our authentic turning rather than settle for a superficial adjustment or temporary remorse. Shallow, hurried, untested repentance is of no value. It's of no value to the individual who sins or to the local church with which the Lord has an issue. Inauthentic repentance will be unhelpful to us and unsatisfactory to our Lord. May God grant us the kind of repentance that enables us to see our sin for what it is and motivates us to turn from all our wicked ways.

Addressing Corporate Repentance

In corporate repentance the authenticity factor is even more important because the ministry of an entire church is at stake. When a church first discovers unresolved sin in its history or current experience, the Lord calls that church to repent, even as He did five of the seven churches He addressed in Revelation 2-3. Corporate sin demands bodily attention. When we see pain in the history of a church, we look for the root cause, because whatever happened there is what hinders revival and God's blessing on that church. This much is review. The question is: How do we move on to experience God's blessing again?

> "The way to blessing is through the gate of repentance."

The way to blessing is through the gate of repentance. There are three items that must be addressed to properly result in corporate repentance and regain God's blessing on a congregation: 1) We need to see how unresolved sin in the history of a church limits the ministry effectiveness of our church. 2) We need to understand how leaders can mediate before God and deal with the sins that have occurred in the history of our church. 3) We need to determine how we should repent on behalf of those whose sin infected the body but may be no longer present or may be unwilling to repent.

The first two issues above can be illustrated from a story about David and Saul found in 2 Samuel 21:1-14. Take a moment to become familiar with the following account from the life of David:

> [1] Now there was a famine in the days of David for three years, year after year; and David sought the presence of the LORD. And the LORD said, "It is for Saul and his bloody house, because he put the Gibeonites to death." [2] So the king called the Gibeonites and spoke to them (now the Gibeonites were

not of the sons of Israel but of the remnant of the Amorites, and the sons of Israel made a covenant with them, but Saul had sought to kill them in his zeal for the sons of Israel and Judah).

[3] Thus David said to the Gibeonites, "What should I do for you? And how can I make atonement that you may bless the inheritance of the LORD?" [4] Then the Gibeonites said to him, "We have no concern of silver or gold with Saul or his house, nor is it for us to put any man to death in Israel." And he said, "I will do for you whatever you say." [5] So they said to the king, "The man who consumed us and who planned to exterminate us from remaining within any border of Israel, [6] let seven men from his sons be given to us, and we will hang them before the LORD in Gibeah of Saul, the chosen of the LORD." And the king said, "I will give them."

[7] But the king spared Mephibosheth, the son of Jonathan the son of Saul, because of the oath of the LORD which was between them, between David and Saul's son Jonathan. [8] So the king took the two sons of Rizpah the daughter of Aiah, Armoni and Mephibosheth whom she had borne to Saul, and the five sons of Merab the daughter of Saul, whom she had borne to Adriel the son of Barzillai the Meholathite. [9] Then he gave them into the hands of the Gibeonites, and they hanged them in the mountain before the LORD, so that the seven of them fell together; and they were put to death in the first days of harvest at the beginning of barley harvest.

[10] And Rizpah the daughter of Aiah took sackcloth and spread it for herself on the rock, from the beginning of harvest until it rained on them from the sky; and she allowed neither the birds of the sky to rest on them by day nor the beasts of the field by night. [11] When it was told David what Rizpah the daughter of Aiah, the concubine of Saul, had done, [12] then David went and took the bones of Saul and the bones of Jonathan his son from the men of Jabesh-gilead, who had stolen them from the open square of Beth-shan, where the Philistines had hanged them on the day the Philistines struck down Saul in Gilboa.

[13] He brought up the bones of Saul and the bones of Jonathan his son from there, and they gathered the bones of those who had been hanged. [14] They buried the bones of Saul and Jonathan his son in the country of Benjamin in Zela, in the grave of Kish his father; thus they did all that the king commanded, and after that God was moved by prayer for the land.

Do you remember who the Gibeonites were? Joshua met these tricky folks when in the midst of conquering Canaan (See Joshua 9). They portrayed themselves as a people from a land far, far away. Because Joshua and his leaders failed to ask the Lord for discernment, they established a peace covenant with them, though they lived just down the road. The Gibeonites' ruse secured their protection.

Though the agreement was made under a false pretense, God required that Joshua and the people honor the agreement nonetheless. The Gibeonites became the servants of the Israelites but they gained their lives in the process.

Many generations later Saul determined to destroy the Gibeonites (2 Samuel 21). We are not told his reasons explicitly except that he was "zealous for the sons of Israel." Did he harbor a grudge toward them for some reason? We just don't know, but God took note when Saul set out to exterminate them from Israel. One writer refers to his action as "ethnic cleansing." Saul's actions were in violation of God's command not to deal deceitfully with foreigners living among Israel and the covenant Joshua made with them (Deut. 27:19). [81]

We learn several things about how God works with Israel corporately in 2 Samuel 21. These observations have analogies to the way God works with all corporate entities, including the local church. 1 Corinthians 10:6 makes it plain, *"Now these things happened [to Israel] as examples for us . . ."* Israel's example warns us of potential missteps in our experience. Israel suffered discipline corporately, and as such their corporate example stands as a warning for the Church and for local churches.

There are ten key observations of significance to us here:

1. There was a famine in Israel at this time. More significantly, there was a *pattern* to the famine: *"There was a famine for three years, year after year"* (21:1). Multiple seasons of famine hit the nation, corporate pain repeating itself. If we were in Israel at the time we might chalk up one famine to bad seed, another to locusts, but the third? If we had a couple of good years mixed in among a few bad ones, we might not give it a second thought. But three successive years? We'd begin to wonder, "What's going on here? Lord do you have something against us?" We might question like Gideon did, *"If the Lord is with us, why has all this happened to us?"* (Judges 6:13) That's just the question God wanted the pain to cause the Israelites to ask.

2. David sought the Lord as to the cause of the famine. *"And David sought the presence of the Lord"* (vs.1). David did not say to himself, "Hmmm . . . the weather has been bad lately and the national economy is being affected – well, these things happen." David understood the nature of Divine metamessages through corporate pain. David had the wisdom to see the change in national prosperity as a time to seek the Lord. God caused pain to the corporate body of

Israel and David got the message. May we be so wise!

3. God told David the reason for the famine. When David sought the Lord, the Lord revealed the root of the problem. God told him, "*It is for Saul and his bloody house, because he put the Gibeonites to death.*" Note that the reason Israel suffered famine had nothing to do with David! The problem occurred in his *predecessor's* administration. The perpetrator of the offense was gone from the scene, dead! The implications of these facts are astounding. They imply that sins in the history of a corporate entity hinder God's blessing on them decades into the future. They reveal that, though the offense was perpetrated by a previous office holder, the current office holder inherits responsibility for the problem before God!

Let that sink in as it relates to the church (or denomination) you lead. The ministry frustration your church faces may be unrelated to its *current* pastor, staff, or, board! You may have inherited a set of problems about which you had no clue. If you fail to interpret the repeated episodes of pain as symptoms of an unresolved sin in your church's history, then you doom yourself to minister amidst an ongoing, divinely-caused famine. This means little or no fruit no matter how much effort you put in, and it may not even be your fault though everyone might be blaming you!

God did not play cat and mouse with David when David asked Him the reason for the corporate pain. A review of state records could have revealed Saul's unjustified actions and his drive to annihilate the Gibeonites. Anyone who knew how God felt about covenants would realize that Saul's actions caused a major problem in Israel's relationship with God.

If a similar issue exists in the history of your church and is causing present pain, God will not hide it from you. This is not spiritual guess-work. The history of your church will reveal what the Lord has against your congregation. What would the Lord say to your church? What would He affirm and commend? What challenges would He note that you have overcome? About what would He say, "*But I have this against you?*" If you have corporate pain, then there is something. Listen to what the Lord has been saying to your church. He will not hide it.

4. The famine was a *symptom* of the root problem. The real problem God had was Saul's violation of an ancient covenant between the Israelites and the Gibeonites. This is problematic for a couple of reasons.

First, God takes the violations of covenants seriously, even if we are unaware or ignorant of their existence. How well has the former leadership stuck to your church's constitution? The constitution and bylaws of a church are a covenant document. Do you know how well things were kept before you arrived in your church? When you read old board records, do you ever wonder what motivated some of the decisions and commitments they made? Did they ever bypass the church constitution to do so? It could be possible that your current problems are tied to violations in those areas. People may cause trouble by "moving an ancient boundary" even if it is unknown to them.

The second problem relates to the question of how to correctly interpret a crisis or crises in your church. David would have missed the message if he decided instead to institute a "Future Farmers of Israel" program to improve farming techniques. His efforts would also have been misguided if he chose to increase his country's imports of produce from nearby nations. This is just the kind of thing leaders of churches do with their corporate pain instead of asking God what it's about.

Be careful of focusing on the *apparent* problem and missing the *real* problem. Most middle-aged men would panic if a jolt of sharp pain paralyzed their left arm. Such pain in that location could speak of a far more serious problem. However, if a guy thinks he has a strained muscle in his left arm instead of possibly having a coronary, he may settle for a dangerous misdiagnosis. Sometimes a strained muscle is just that, but if the pain reoccurs or grows in intensity, it's time to head to the emergency room. In our church history, the key diagnostic question is: do we see a *pattern* of pain "year after year" or are we looking at an individual spasm in need of treatment?

5. Though Saul's sin appeared to be done for the right reasons, God saw it as sin. His is the only opinion that matters. 2 Samuel 21:2 touches on Saul's motivation for killing the Gibeonites: "*Saul had sought to kill them in his zeal for the sons of Israel and Judah.*" Saul was a patriot! Zeal mixed with nationalism played a role in wanting to rid God's land of these "foreigners." Saul championed the Israelite cause and felt justified. He could easily substantiate his reasons. King Saul's actions appeared right to him at the time. God obviously saw things differently.

How does this relate to the way God deals with corporate entities today? Oftentimes leaders have said things, done things, and made decisions that appeared correct to them at the time. Their policies sounded perfectly reasonable, even good, at the time they were implemented. Justifications could be marshaled to prove it.

However, God was not consulted for His opinion. There may be things in the history of your organization or church that the enactors never saw as inappropriate. In their zeal for some issue that touched the life of the church, they acted impetuously like Saul and assumed God's blessing on what they did without ever asking Him. Perhaps these decision-makers were a product of their culture and the actions they took reflected their day rather than God's perspective on the issue in question. Race issues and segregated churches in the South are an example of this, a wound not yet fully rectified. All the while they were clueless that they offended God and brought judgment on their corporate body.

I know of one church that tolerated the presence of a high-ranking Ku Klux Klan leader. Perhaps subtle pride that the imperial wizard attended their church gave them a sense of satisfaction. But the church leaders' decision to accept this man without rebuke in the congregation was fostered more by cultural values than biblical ones. At the time they would have thought their disposition toward this individual was completely appropriate. Now that time has past. What did God think at the time they chose to assimilate this man into the church without rebuke? They, like Saul, thought they were doing the right thing at the time. God's response to Saul's actions should give pause to all those in local church leadership. God holds us accountable for sinful decisions we thought were proper at the time but were not God's intent.

6. God hindered the nation until David addressed the root problem. We cannot miss that the famine continued until David rectified the broken covenant with the Gibeonites. When something sinful occurs in the *history* of a group, we cannot say it is irrelevant to that body's *present or future*. Time does not make the sin go away before God. There is a great temptation to say, "What's past is past" or "Why do we need to revisit such painful sagas in the history of our church?" or "What good is it to bring that stuff up?"

The crux of the story of the Gibeonites is that, unless a corporate body addresses those issues that have offended God, God will hinder their ministry. They enter into a period of "famine;" it may be a famine of spiritual fruit or unity or loving relationships among those in the body. The years of famine may vary in their scope but, if left unconfessed and unrectified, the famine will continue.

7. David sought to make restitution on behalf of the nation. In verses 3-4, David asks, "*What should I do for you? And how can I make atonement . . .*" He begins to move toward a solution to Saul's sin against the Gibeonites. This is also the starting point for sin we find in the history of our churches. David's question, "*How can I make atonement?*" demonstrates that spiritual leaders have authority to act as mediators between God, offended people, and the sins of the congregation's history. Mediatorial authority means that leaders have the ability to act in God's name as it relates to righting wrongs in the history of a church. "Spiritual authorities have a God-given right to act in God's name. The church leaders act and speak to make things right with God through corporate confession and restitution on behalf of the congregation."[82] We'll discuss mediatorial authority in a section all its own, but in answer to our question posed earlier, "How does a church repent?" we learn from David's example that leaders can make things right before God and others on behalf of the corporate body.

8. David sought to restore God's blessing on Israel. In verse 3, David goes on to say: "*that you may bless the inheritance of the Lord.*" David knows that if the remaining Gibeonites see the restitution as sufficient, they will bless the nation. And if they bless it, then so will God. In this we see the difference between God's *blessing* and God's *presence* with them. God has still dwelt in their midst as a nation, otherwise God would have remained silent when David sought Him. But God's *blessing* was another matter. In the same way a church may still have God's presence while lacking a clear experience of His blessing.

> "Leaders can make things right before God and others on behalf of the corporate body."

Many think that they are enjoying God's blessing when in reality they are weakly going through the motions of doing church. They operate in default mode with a minimum of spiritual power. When a vacuum line in my car's air conditioning broke, the AC defaulted to the defrost vents. The AC still "functioned" but not in a way that I could enjoy the full benefit. I could say I enjoyed a minimal amount of blessing blowing through the vents. Once repaired, I enjoyed the full force of the cold air again. The Lord's presence is always with us until He removes our lampstand utterly as a church. In the meantime the fullness of His blessing gets inhibited by our corporate sin. The question is: are we now enjoying the fullness of His blessing?

9. Once acts of restitution and contrition were made, God heard the prayers for the land. The story concludes in vs. 14: "*after that God was moved by entreaty for the land.*" It seems gruesome to us that the lives of seven young men were sacrificed to satisfy the remaining Gibeonites and that God accepted this act as atonement for the nation's sin. The grandsons of Saul ended up paying for the offense of Saul and served as just restitution for the remaining Gibeonites. Justice was served.

---

[82] Quick, *Church and Community* Exegesis 16.

For our purposes, when we discover sin in the history of our church that may have hurt unjustly a former pastor, lay leader or a group of people, we should also be ready to make restitution. We may not realize the price paid by those who suffered because of some unrighteous act in a church's past. But when that price comes to light, any apology issued should include just restitution that demonstrates the church's desire to make things right. Words may not be enough to satisfy God's justice.

Until David took these steps of restitution, the Lord closed His ears to the people's entreaties. Imagine God maintains a complaint against a local church and the membership prays for relief from the difficulties they keep facing. God sends those difficulties to get them to seek His face regarding their offensive behavior. The dear saints, however, pray merely for relief from the pain which divine discipline imposed on them. Have they properly discerned God's will in this case? No, they pray the wrong prayer. The more appropriate prayer for the occasion would be, "Lord what's the real nature of the problems we are facing?" Not until they discover and address the true nature of their situation, will God hear their prayer.

10. David still treated Saul's memory with respect, recognizing him as God's anointed leader though he was guilty of the sin which caused their pain. In vss. 10-14, we see how David honored Saul, Jonathan and the others, even though they were dead and gone. He carefully gathered the bones of these men and gave them a proper burial. I believe David honored Saul in life and in death for the same reason. He did not merely honor the individual, but he also honored the office Saul held. The office was worthy of honor and that honor continued in death. David saw Saul as the Lord's anointed king and, if he diminished Saul or his office, David would have diminished the One who placed Saul in the office.

What bearing does this have on corporate repentance as it relates to the local church? When we examine the history of our church, we need to be careful not to diminish any leader or person whose sin infected the body. Christ died for them and they belong to Him! All authority comes from God (Romans 13), and if an individual misuses the authority associated with their spiritual role, that misuse must be addressed, but we must also show sensitivity in our treatment of the individual. They may have been very imperfect, but for the sake of the *office* we need to show respect for the office holder in spite of his or her faults.

Some former leader in your church may have contributed to the problems with which you now wrestle. Remember David's example and remember your vulnerability to the same kind of sin. When you discover the skeleton in your church's closet, be careful how you treat those bones!

David and Saul in Summary

Responsibility for sin follows the office not merely the office holder. Time alone does not heal all wounds nor cover sin in the history of a church. Current leaders can act as a mediatorial authority on behalf of a congregation's past sin. It is mediatorial authority that allows current leaders to rectify the sins of the past.

Mediatorial Authority

This amazing authority God gives to leaders allows them to act on behalf of the congregation before God. Mediatorial authority is a God-given right to mediate disputes between God and His people. We see this in the previous example of David and the Gibeonites. Leaders can repent and rectify issues before God on behalf of the body they represent. When one asks, "How does a congregation as a *body* repent before God?" the answer lies in the fact that a church's authorities have the right to do so on behalf of the congregation.

We see the opposite side of mediatorial authority illustrated in the case of the man living in open immorality described in 1 Corinthians 5. Paul's conclusion on the matter was: *"For I, on my part, though absent in body but present in spirit, have already judged him who has so committed this as though I were present."* Paul assumes the authority to represent God to the congregation. Mediatorial authority works both ways, representing the congregation to God but also God to the congregation. Paul took action in keeping with the God-given authority of his office. He exercised God's authority over a church conflict even when he was not physically present at the church.

To bypass, deceive or frustrate the authority of church leaders is to resist God's authority. Acts has several illustrations of this. For instance, Peter's words to Ananias and Sapphira when he says to them in Acts 5, *"You have not lied to men but to God,"* is an example of Peter using his God-given authority to set things right before God. It also demonstrates the perpetrator's lack of appreciation for mediatorial authority. Peter pronounced effective judgment on them. Such mediatorial authority binds human leaders closely with God's authority in order to settle congregational matters before God.

Acts 6:1-7 describes the conflict over the care of Jewish widows of Hellenistic background. The Apostles exercised their authority to solve the dispute by delegating the task of caring for these ladies to seven specially selected deacons.

The twelve arbitrated a solution based on their God-given authority. Mediatorial authority can resolve conflicts between parties within the church, but, by resolving this, they also resolve an inequity that God found displeasing. The apostles thus use their mediatorial authority to make things right before God.

In Acts 13:1-3, mediatorial authority allows the leaders to act on behalf of the people before God. In the account of the setting apart of Barnabas and Saul for their missionary work, the leaders of the church at Antioch lay hands on them and confirm the leading of the Holy Spirit. In effect they act as God's agents to confirm and confer the calling of God on His chosen instruments. This is the principle which operates in ordination.

The Sins of the Fathers

Jesus alludes to the tremendous danger of leaders failing to exercise mediatorial authority in Matthew 23:29-32:

> "Woe to you, scribes and Pharisees, hypocrites! For you build the tombs of the prophets and adorn the monuments of the righteous, and say, 'If we had been living in the days of our fathers, we would not have been partners with them in shedding the blood of the prophets.' So you testify against yourselves, that you are sons of those who murdered the prophets. Fill up, then, the measure of the guilt of your fathers."

The Pharisees had convinced themselves they could never do anything like their fathers did, yet Jesus said they were the "*sons of those who murdered the prophets.*" The Pharisees may have wanted to disassociate themselves from the sinful actions of their ancestors but Jesus saw an unbroken connection between them and those murderers.

If the Pharisees had sensitivity to their own sinfulness, they would have known their potential for repeating the sins of their fathers. Their lack of humility desensitized them from feeling the full weight of the sin in their heritage. If they had understood, they might have sought to rectify those sins before God, or at least felt the shame of them. Instead, they sought to prove they were different from their fathers' sin through symbolic acts of adorning the monuments of the righteous and building tombs for the prophets. Their denial actually set them up to repeat the family pattern.

Eventually the Pharisees do far worse than their fathers when they crucify Christ. When Jesus said to them, "*Fill up, then, the measure of the guilt of your fathers,*"

He foresaw the Pharisees would not escape their "family tradition" even though they utterly denied that possibility. The Pharisees' hypocrisy drove them to do the very things they condemned![83]

Unless they take responsibility for the sins of the fathers, recognizing the sin is in their own hearts too, the pattern continues and their sons and their sons' sons will keep filling up the guilt. Mediatorial authority allows us to break the patterns of sinful behavior we may be inheriting from those who have gone before us. It frees us from blindly repeating their mistakes.

The implication for churches is huge. If you likewise see patterns of sin in the history of your church, don't think or say "Thank God we are not like those folk who did those things!" If you do, the sin will continue until someone takes responsibility and exercises mediatorial authority to rectify the issue(s) before the Lord.

This need to repent on behalf of those who have sinned before us is not a new idea. One early American preacher, Benjamin Coleman, preached a sermon in 1716 titled, "*Our Father's Sins and Ours.*" His text was Psalm 106:6 *"We have sinned with our fathers; we have committed iniquity; we have done wickedly."* Consider the following excerpt:

> "That we should mourn for our own personal sins in the first place, you will easily acknowledge . . . But we must mourn for the sins of others together with our own. Sin ought to grieve us wherever we see it . . . What better reverence can we show unto our Father in heaven while we go backward, like the blushing sons of Noah, drawing a covering over our earthly parents' nakedness . . . The hatred of sin which God requires in us must be impartial because it is based on the honor of God. Those that justify sin in relatives and close friends which they condemn in others demonstrate their great distance from a right understanding and practice of this doctrine."[84]

Exercising mediatorial authority to repent of the sins of those who preceded you

---

[83] Samuel Coleman shares these comments, ". . . they treated the prophets in their day just as their fathers had done long before; they were impenitent and obstinate in sin just as their fathers had been under the ministry of former prophets; they were of the same persecuting spirit as their fathers; thus their fathers' sin was theirs, and both were to be confessed in the same breath. It is part of the folly of the Pharisees and an evidence of their hypocrisy that they could confess their father's persecution of the prophets and not discern their own." (See Roberts, Sanctify the Congregation 150)

[84] Ibid 149-150.

in leadership, places a special burden on Christian leaders. It is not enough to have a "here and now perspective" on the health of your church. What has gone on in the past of your church is very much alive before our living Lord. If you lead in ignorance of what went on or think "digging up dirt" is not worth rocking the church boat to address, don't be surprised to find your ministry hindered. You should not be shocked to find the Spirit of God grieving. He's grieving because you won't. Your leadership will reflect that lack of discernment and failure to seek the Lord.

Identificational Repentance

We need to explore how repentance can take place on behalf of those whose sin infected the body but are no longer present or are present but unwilling to repent. I once served as interim pastor in a small suburban church. My second Sunday, one of the older saints came up after the service and rehearsed the painful details of a previous pastor who, because of moral failure, left the church wounded. The event occurred twenty-five years earlier but the pain was still fresh.

Unrepentant and defiant, this superbly gifted yet fallen pastor refused to be held accountable for his deeds. He took the church from 250 members down to 30 in twelve months. He also left the shrunken congregation saddled with a debt of $300,000. How would you like to have been one of the thirty people left holding that bag? Being unrepentant and no longer associated with the church, how do you address the devastating trail of tears and sin he left behind?

Identificational repentance allows one individual to stand in the place of another and ask forgiveness in the offender's place. We see this principle unfold in several Old Testament passages. In Daniel 9:1-20, Daniel confesses the sins of his people as if they were his own. He brings the sins of those who had gone before him to the Lord: "*So I gave my attention to the Lord God to seek Him by prayer and supplications, with fasting, sackcloth and ashes and I prayed . . . we have sinned, committed iniquity, acted wickedly, and rebelled, even turning aside from thy commandments and ordinances . . . Open shame belongs to us, O Lord, to our kings, our princes, and our fathers, because we have sinned against Thee . . .*"

The response from heaven was almost immediate. The angel Gabriel appeared *while Daniel was praying* to give Daniel further understanding. When as church leaders we take responsibility for the transgressions of those whose sin lingers in our midst, we immediately affect heaven's disposition toward us.

We see Ezra functioning similarly in Ezra 9:5-15, "*But at the evening offering I arose from my humiliation, even with my garment and my robe torn, and I fell on my knees and stretched out my hands to the Lord my God; and I said, 'O my God, I am ashamed and embarrassed to lift up my face to Thee, my God, for* **our** *iniquities have risen above* **our** *heads, and* **our** *guilt has grown even to the heavens. Since the days of* **our** *fathers to this day* **we** *have been in great guilt, and on account of* **our** *iniquities we,* **our** *kings and* **our** *priests have been given into the hand of the kings of the land . . .'"*

Ezra confesses the nation's sin as if it were his own. He stands in the place of those whose sin led them into captivity and *associates* himself rather than separates himself from their sin. He *owns* it. He recognizes his own potential for sin and failure so it is not faked. He acknowledges the sins of a group to which he belongs. It is a crucial role of leadership.

Nehemiah also personally accepts responsibility for the sins of his fathers as he confesses them before the Lord in Nehemiah 1:4-7. *"Now it came about when I heard these words, I sat down and wept and mourned for days; and I was fasting and praying before the God of heaven. And I said, 'I beseech Thee O Lord God of heaven, the great and awesome God, who preserves the covenant and lovingkindness for those who love Him and keep His commandments, let Thine ear now be attentive and Thine eyes open to hear the prayer of Thy servant which I am praying before Thee now, day and night,* **on behalf of the sons of Israel** *Thy servants,* **confessing the sins of the sons of Israel** *which* **we** *have sinned against Thee;* **I and my father's house have sinned.** **We** *have acted very corruptly against Thee . . .'"*

Sin's damage may have been done in the past but God has not left us without a solution in the present. Through identificational repentance, a ministry leader admits the sins of the past as if he were among those who shared in them. John Dawson writes in his book, *Healing America's Wounds*, "Nehemiah and the families with him assembled themselves before the Lord with fasting, in sackcloth and with dust on their heads. Though they were just a remnant, they completely identified with their nation and its history. *'Then those of Israelite lineage separated themselves from all foreigners; and they stood and confessed their sins and the iniquities of their fathers'* (Neh. 9:2 NKJV). When we ask for God's mercy on others, we should never say, 'How could they do such a thing?' We know exactly how they could do it, because the potential for the worst evil lies within each one of us, apart from God's saving grace and the life of Christ within us." [85]

---

[85] Dawson 96.

By recognizing our susceptibility to the same deeds, we can stand in the place of those who are no longer available or who are unwilling to do so and honestly confess. Quick writes, "In identificational repentance, I recognize how I identify or am identified with the perpetrator(s) of an injustice or injury. Because I am identified with him/her, I can stand in their place and shoulder the responsibility they never did."[86]

In the church where a previous pastor's immorality and unrepentant desertion wounded the church, I stood before the congregation during a special service of corporate repentance and said, "The pastor, who caused so much pain that it lingers to this day, is no longer here. He is unwilling to admit fault. But I stand before you as a pastor who is just as capable of the same sin and pain he caused. I know that in the course of my ministry, I have wounded people too. Would you forgive me in his place before the Lord?" It was simple and heartfelt; no mere reading of a dry liturgy, no emotional manipulation. In that moment, the congregation's heart opened and they were willing to forgive and let go of the wound which hindered them. They began to enjoy a time of freedom after a quarter century of pain.

Summary

Authentic repentance on a corporate level restores the energies of a local church. It removes the stains that have accumulated on the Bride of Christ and restores a glistening radiance to her countenance. The corporate conscience gets cleansed and God's blessing begins to flow immediately. Corporate repentance takes great courage to pursue but its rewards are equal to the effort. Real leadership starts by facing the problems of the past and making them right before the Lord and with those wounded.

---

[86] Quick, *Healing the Heart of Your Church* 75

Chapter Eight

then will I hear from heaven and forgive their sin and heal their land

"Can it happen again? You ask? The answer is, positively, yes. For the Holy Spirit is as powerful today as He was on the day of Pentecost. All He waits for is the church, made up of men and women who are prepared to quit grieving Him and quenching Him in order that He might fill and overflow in revival blessing . . ."
- Stephen Olford

"John Davidson of Prestonpans, Scotland became burdened for the welfare of his beloved church and gave expression of concern at the Synod of Fife in 1593 and the Assembly in 1594. His presbytery of Haddington joined with him in petitioning the General Assembly of the Church to set aside time for a Solemn Assembly at the annual meeting of 1596. The Assembly met at St. Giles Cathedral, Edinburgh in March. A very thorough catalogue of sins was prepared which covered the misdeeds of every class of persons from the King on down to the meanest subjects. More space was given to the sins of ministers than to the wickedness of all other classes put together. The Solemn Assembly occurred on the Tuesday of the second week of the General Assembly and some 400 men, mostly ministers participated . . . The Holy Spirit of God came down and the ancient Cathedral Church resounded with the sobs and cries of hundreds of ministers humbling themselves before God on the dirt floor. The spirit of corporate repentance was carried into all the Presbyteries and the revival of 1596 followed."[87]

This snippet of Scottish Presbyterian history illustrates the impact of a service of corporate repentance. Sometimes called a "Repentance Service" or a "Reconciliation Service" or a "Corporate Renewal Service," biblically it is termed a "Solemn Assembly".[88]

The final phrase of 2 Chronicles 7:14 says, *"then will I hear from heaven and will forgive their sin and will heal their land."* I want to focus on just one key word: "then." This little word "then" is the fulcrum on which the promise of revival rests. If revival is conditioned upon the requirements we have investigated to this point, when is revival triggered? When is this *"then"*?

"Then" refers to the point in time when God's attitude and disposition toward His people changes. In that moment, a fresh encounter occurs with God's Spirit which results in a recovery of God's blessing. The occasion under which God unleashes His blessing is an assembly where God's people right their relationship with God. That event where we transact such serious spiritual business is known as a Solemn Assembly.

A Solemn Assembly gives leaders and the rest of the church an opportunity to remedy the sins and wounds in the history of their church. It's where individuals address personal sin as well.
- It is the place where the body's leaders exercise their mediatorial authority and identificational repentance before God.
- It allows participation in repentance among the congregation.
- It gives the congregation a specific time and date to mark the changes they seek in their corporate behavior.
- It makes a collective statement of sorrow for the sinful past before God.
- It encourages congregational forgiveness and healing as the church humbles itself before the Lord.
- It presents an opportunity to enter into a corporate covenant with God as a church aspires to move in a new direction.

Solemn Assemblies provide more than a *theoretical* solution to sin. It's *the way* God's people got right with Him in the Bible. It's also the way our spiritual forefathers did it in American history. Local churches today are following this model with near instant results. The church atmosphere and sense of corporate

---

[87] Roberts, *Sanctify the Congregation* 12.
[88] See the Facilitator's Guide for *Healing the Heart of Your Church*, by Barnard and Quick, ChurchSmart Resources (2008).

106

blessing change almost immediately when church leaders follow this Divine prescription for making things right.

In this chapter we will explore the elements found in Solemn Assemblies outlined in the Scriptures. We will also look at their roots in American history. We want to describe several modern examples of Solemn Assemblies and the way they impacted their congregations. Finally, we will examine some warnings related to use of Solemn Assemblies and give the reader balanced expectations of what corporate revival can and can't do.

Biblical Elements of Solemn Assemblies

The examples we read about in the Old Testament carry weight and relevance for New Testament believers. Romans 15:4 says, *"For whatever was written in earlier times was written for our instruction, that through perseverance and the encouragement of the Scriptures we might have hope."* We find a viable solution to unresolved sin and wounds in the Old Testament Solemn Assembly. God has provided a remedy in His mercy.

The role of Solemn Assemblies is established early in the writings of Moses. Leviticus 23 describes such "holy convocations" as times of humility, special offerings, national atonement, and complete dedication to the things of God. 2 Chronicles 7:14, the very promise of revival we have made our focus, occurred in answer to Solomon's prayer during a Solemn Assembly at the dedication of the Temple.

Solemn Assemblies were special times prescribed by God for His people to reset their relationship with Him and address their faults and failings. It provided an opportunity to refresh and renew their relationship with God.

Ezra and the Problem of Intermarriage

We find the most detailed example of a Solemn Assembly in the book of Ezra. From this example we see the various elements that go into the making of an Assembly. Ezra faced an "engaging" problem. It came to his attention that some of the exiles that returned to replant the nation had started to intermarry with women from neighboring peoples. This breach of covenant faithfulness threatened to undo God's blessing on the restart nation. Ezra did not turn a blind eye, nor relax God's standards, nor passively say, "What's done is done, we'll have to move on from here." Rather, in Ezra 9, he tore his clothes in grief and cried out on behalf of God's people. Satan had planted the seeds of sin and compromise all over again, the very things that had caused their exile in the first place.

Ezra put the problem in clear spiritual perspective when he said, *"But now for a brief moment grace has been shown from the Lord our God, to leave us an escaped remnant and to give us a peg in His holy place, that our God may enlighten our eyes and grant us a little reviving in our bondage . . . And now, our God, what shall we say after this for we have forsaken Thy commandments . . ."* (Ezra 9:8, 10).

Ezra's grief spread among the godly people of Israel. As their hearts broke, they called a Solemn Assembly in Jerusalem. Along with Ezra, the leaders and the elders of Israel agreed to this course of action. In the midst of pouring rain, the vast assembly gathered to acknowledge the sin infecting their nation and to resolve the matter before the Lord.

Several things are evident in this Solemn Assembly. First and foremost we discover the element of hope. Shecaniah says in Ezra 10:2, *"We have been unfaithful to our God, and have married foreign women from the people of the land; yet now there is **hope** for Israel in spite of this."* I like Shecaniah because he saw beyond God's judgment to God's mercy. When we discover our failures as a church, we should grieve appropriately but not as those who have no hope. We need not be discouraged to the point of despair. God makes a way to restoration from the sin that may have snared us as a church. God made a way for Israel and He makes a way for us too. No sin is beyond the scope of God's grace, even when it defiles the entire body of a church. We call for a Solemn Assembly in order to be cleansed of our sin through corporate confession and seek to restore God's blessing on our congregation. God promises to restore our blessing if we take seriously how we have fallen and repent (Rev. 2:5, 6). That is what revival is all about. When we decide to have a Solemn Assembly, like the Israelites in Ezra's day we should do so with the hopeful anticipation that, as we humble ourselves and turn from our wicked ways, God will once again bless us.

Secondly, Shecaniah outlines another element of Solemn Assemblies when he says in 10:3, *"So now let us make a **covenant** with our God to put away all the wives and their children, according to the counsel of my lord and those who tremble at the commandment of our God."* Solemn Assemblies should be times when we renew our commitment to follow the Lord as a body. Developing a corporate covenant helps us articulate the behaviors that displeased the Lord in the first place and allows us to promise to avoid those things and make commitments to aspire to better things in the future. Identify the specific issues that Christ had against you as you reviewed the history of your church. That should be the starting place for developing your corporate covenant. What was the original purpose of the founders of your church from which you may have departed? That too might be a place to start. These questions form the basis of the corporate covenant you formulate.

To give you an idea of what a corporate covenant might look like, one church wrote the following after a careful review of their church's history. They used this covenant as one aspect of the Solemn Assembly to address unresolved sin in the history of their church. Each statement in their covenant reflected an underlying negative tendency identified in the history of their church. The negative tendencies are included here to put the positive statements in proper context.

Sample Corporate Covenant

1. **We aspire to be a unified fully functional church body for God through clearly defined avenues of communication.**
   (Negative tendency: A lack of open communication and cases of individual offense in the body.)

2. **We will demonstrate a commitment to each other that takes precedence over conflict.**
   (Negative tendency: A tendency to leave when we don't like what is happening, running from conflict.)

3. **When the Holy Spirit is leading us into a faith situation we will pursue it.**
   (Negative Tendency: A tendency to play it safe, slow reaction to opportunities for growth.)

4. **We as church leaders will pursue open, transparent, two way communication in the relationship with our pastor.**
   (Negative tendency: A tendency not to talk about major problems especially in relation to the pastor.)

5. **We will protect the integrity of this ministry through mutual accountability as church leaders.**
   (Negative tendency: un-remedied pastoral sin and weak lay leadership.)

6. **If we fail in any of these aspects we will acknowledge it before God and seek reconciliation with God and the Body of Christ.**
   (Acknowledges the possibility of failure as we grow and mature in these commitments and what we will do about it if we fail in one way or another.)

I find point number six especially significant. A corporate covenant and a Solemn Assembly cannot guarantee to prevent regressive behavior. The covenant document gives a church a standard to which they can aspire, but it also acknowledges the possibility of human weakness and failure as they seek to change their corporate behavior. They won't be perfect, but they will keep trying. We'll talk about corporate regression later, but for now it is important to see how a corporate covenant can set a new course for the church to follow.

A third element of Solemn Assemblies which shows up in the Ezra account is *confession*. Ezra instructs the whole assembly in 10:11, "*Now, therefore, make* **confession** *to the Lord God of your fathers . . .*" To their credit, they were willing to confess the sin as if it were their own. They saw the sin of the men who married foreign women as their own responsibility. The guilty individuals had not been specifically identified, but the congregation understood that, because of their corporate standing before God as a body, they shared the perpetrators' guilt.

They were also willing to let the leadership of the congregation represent them before God in relationship to their sin. The congregation's wise input follows, "*Then the assembly answered and said in a loud voice, 'That's right! As you have said, so it is our duty to do. But there are many people, it is the rainy season, and we are not able to stand in the open. Nor can the task be done in one or two days, for we have transgressed greatly in this matter.* **Let our leaders represent the whole assembly** *. . .*" (Ezra 10:12-14). This is the role of mediatorial authority in the setting of the Solemn Assembly. Spiritual leadership has the authority to make things right before God on behalf of the congregation, to speak to God on their behalf. Any Solemn Assembly held today should be led by the church's recognized/appointed leaders. They have authority from God to make matters right before Him, things that have hindered His blessing on the congregation. Thus church leaders should be thoroughly involved in the planning and execution of the Solemn Assembly, especially in confessing their corporate sin.

Next we see the **resolution** of the problem. They undertake an investigation to identify those who had married foreign women. This discipline was necessary to make things right before God. Dealing with the tangle of relationships between an Israelite husband, a foreign wife, and their children would have been tough to say the least. It is no less difficult to deal with the discipline problems we have ignored in our churches. No one wants to make things right if they don't have to. Yet to confess without resolving the issues we confess in a godly way stops short of authentic repentance. Be prepared to address your substantive issues before God in preparation for and in conclusion of a Solemn Assembly. The last thing any church wants to do is go through the motions of confession without correction of the problems at hand. That kind of solution is insufficient to restore God's blessing.

Interestingly, but not surprisingly, another issue we see is *resistance* to the conclusions drawn by the leadership in a Solemn Assembly. We read in Ezra 10:15, "*Only Jonathan the son of Asahel and Jahzeiah the son of Tikvah opposed this, with Meshullam and Shabbethai the Levite supporting them.*" Not everyone will agree with the conclusions drawn by a church's leadership as it relates to corporate sin. There will be those who are unhappy about addressing long-ignored problems, even if these are the very things that hinder God's blessing. Some will deem it inappropriate to go public with the problems, yet humility calls for tactful public acknowledgment of corporate shortcomings. Some could have interpreted the rainy weather as a sign they should delay or put off their Solemn Assembly. But Ezra and the leaders did not let inclement weather hinder the change they needed in their corporate heart. Those godly people went forward with the Solemn Assembly in spite of the heavy rain and in spite of those who resisted their decision to move forward.

Finally, the Ezra account of a Solemn Assembly includes both *real and symbolic acts of repentance*. Those whose sin infected the nation "*pledged to put away their wives, and being guilty, they offered a ram of the flock for their offense*" (Ezra 10:19). The men who had intermarried with foreign women first pledged to "*put away their wives.*" This was the *real* act of repentance. They had to dissolve the marriages into which they entered. This was proof that they were willing to submit to spiritual authority and the will of God. Superficial repentance stops short of undoing the trouble we have caused because it is too costly or difficult; not so with these men. They dealt with the spiritual compromise they had made.

Symbolic acts were also involved in their repentance. We note that each man offered a ram from his flock as a sacrifice for his offense. This was the *symbolic* payment for his sin and guilt. It would be helpful if the believers who cause their churches trouble always demonstrated the same pliable disposition. Often the sin gets perpetrated by individuals who are unwilling to repent. That's where church discipline should enter and the wayward individuals choose then to flee from godly correction or submit to their discipline and grow from it.

In the account of Ezra's Solemn Assembly, we see the interplay between personal and corporate sin. The actions of individuals led to the nation's guilt before God. The entire nation stood liable in God's sight for this sinful behavior. In the resolution of the problem, the whole nation took responsibility through the mouths of their leaders, and the sinful ones had to correct their hearts and behavior as part of the corporate repentance process. Corporate sin and personal sin are often intertwined. God holds entire bodies of believers accountable for the unrectified historical sin of individuals within those bodies. Solemn Assemblies take responsibility for the decisions, actions and dispositions of those who have wounded or hindered the body of Christ in the past. Until those issues are addressed, the church languishes under the disciplinary hand of God. Fear of a return to being under divine discipline motivated Ezra and the other leaders of the nation to make things right before the situation got worse.

Their example shows us many of the elements of a Solemn Assembly which it is good to contemplate before enacting one. By way of review, they are: 1) the hope that God *will* restore us, 2) a corporate covenant, 3) corporate confession of sin, 4) mediatorial authority, 5) resolution of sin's impact, 6) resistance to the idea of correcting sin, and 7) real and symbolic acts of repentance.

It takes courage. Even godly Ezra needed encouragement to follow through with it. Shecaniah said to Ezra, "*Arise! For this matter is your responsibility, but we will be with you; be courageous and act*" (Ezra 10:4). We pursue these matters because, as leaders, we are stewards of the body of Christ. We want His Bride to be radiant when the Groom arrives. We will find this courage because we have hope that God will once again forgive our sin and will also, as Ezra prays in 9:8, "*grant us a little reviving*."

Prince Street

Prince Street Church in Shippensburg, Pennsylvania held such a Solemn Assembly. They were not making the ministry progress they might normally expect under the hand of God's blessing and the pastor and staff had gone through a number of painful experiences. They examined their history and discovered historical patterns of sin impacted the current ministry of their church. They identified the good that God had done in the past as well as the patterns of pain. In preparation for the service they published a Q & A fact sheet to prepare the congregation for this service. Through it you get a feel for the thought and planning that went into their service.

Prince Street Church
Service of Repentance Q & A Sheet

Q: What is the Scriptural basis for this process?
A: The concept of the Lord of the Church, Jesus, calling His people to repentance

runs throughout the Bible, both Old and New Testaments. But the primary basis for this process comes from the book of Revelation. In chapters 2 and 3, the Lord writes letters to seven churches. Although these churches are made up of a collection of individuals, Jesus writes to them as one unit. In each letter, Jesus shares things He commends, things that are sinful, a call to repentance, and a warning of what would happen if the church refused to repent. Essentially, we have been asking the Lord of the Church, Jesus, to show us what His letter to us would be.

Q: Who made the decision to do this?
A: At each step of the process, the Board was unanimous in every decision that has been made.

Q: Who was involved in the process?
A: All Board and staff members and their spouses were asked to participate. We also specifically invited all ministry staff personnel. We also invited everyone in the congregation to join us for this process. Approximately 30 people participated in the seminar and retreat.

Q: Why can't we just let the past be the past?
A: The Lord of the Church, Jesus, doesn't just forget corporate sin. This is why He disciplined Israel with 40 years of wilderness wandering and 70 years of exile. He offers to forgive, but only if His people come to Him in repentance. Until that happens, sin, and its consequences remain. He forgives us individually when we repent individually, but corporate forgiveness requires corporate repentance.

Q: Why do we have to do this together?
A: The Lord of the Church, Jesus, looks at Prince Street Church as one body. When one sins, it impacts all of us. That's why all of us must repent together.

Q: What's going to happen at the Service of Repentance?
A: We'll begin by celebrating seasons of fruitful ministry and all that Christ has done in our midst by His grace. We'll conclude the service by rededicating ourselves to being the body of Christ. But the majority of the service will include a series of people repenting of sin on behalf of pastors, their wives, lay leaders, and the congregation.

Q: How long will the Service of Repentance take?
A: None of us knows, exactly. We want to get this right. We want to be sure that we have repented of everything the Lord of the Church, Jesus, is calling for us to confess. Therefore, we expect the service to take significantly longer than our

normal worship services.

Q: Will ministry for children be provided?
A: Yes. We are planning to provide children's ministries for infants-5th grade.

Q: Who will be coming to this service?
A: We would like everyone who is a part of Prince Street Church to be part of this service. We have also sent letters of invitation to more than 100 people who we believe may have experienced hurt during their time of being part of Prince Street Church.

Q: What will I be expected to do?
A: The congregation will join together in singing, greeting each other, praying, Scripture and unison readings, and Holy Communion. We will also provide opportunity for each person who desires to do so to hammer a nail into a large wooden cross symbolizing that we find healing in the cross of Christ. But rest assured that no one will be expected to speak who does not wish to do so.

Q: What can I do between now and June 1st?
A: Please join us in praying. Our enemy, Satan, will do everything he can to discourage and divide us. But God's power is greater than anything our enemy can place in our way. If we will keep our eyes fixed on the Lord of the Church, Jesus, we will find healing for Prince Street Church.

Price Street Church's thoughtfulness and preparation evidenced by their Q & A sheet demonstrate their passion to pursue God's blessing on their ministry. We want to see many such congregations work to hear from the Lord and, as Prince Street did, make the necessary course corrections to honor the Lord of the Church and be blessed by Him again.

Solemn Assemblies in American History

Special days of fasting and prayer were the norm in the earliest era of American history. It was not unusual for church leaders to interpret natural disasters as a warning or judgment from God. When people felt themselves under God's disciplinary hand, they scheduled Solemn Assemblies for the purpose of corporate repentance. When you read the sermons pastors preached on these special days of fasting and prayer, you see that early American preachers did not hesitate to recognize corporate pain as God's means to get their attention. They saw a tight connection between their painful events and the disciplinary judgments God inflicted on Israel in the Old Testament. *We* have lost this discernment.

In Richard Owen Roberts one-of-a-kind book, *Sanctify the Congregation*, he assembles the sermons of many early American preachers who called for their people to return to the living God. The following excerpts were taken from sermons they preached on days of humiliation and fasting. These Solemn Assemblies were times when they recognized the downward trends of spirituality evident in the Church and society.

Joseph Rowlandson, of Weathersfield, Connecticut preached a sermon in 1678 titled, *The Possibility of God Forsaking a People*. The message formed the exclamation point on this preacher's life as he died two days later. He preached it on a day set apart for fasting and prayer throughout the colonies. He writes:

> "A people must know that God has forsaken them when He ceases to protect them from their enemies as in times past and does not provide for them as He was generous in doing on earlier occasions . . . How is it with the Churches of Asia – those once famous golden candlesticks? They had epistles of warning written to them. Are they not in a forsaken condition now? As far as we know there is not the trace of a Church to be found among them . . . Here it must be noted that God may exercise a great deal of patience and forbearance toward such as He is about to forsake . . . He is very likely to give them warning and in patience to bear a while with their forwardness, to wait and see if there be any returning to Him before He inflicts this heavy and sharp judgment."[89]

Rowlandson further describes how a church ultimately disappears from a community where God planted it. He notes that, when sin infects the body of Christ, God sends divine judgments on His people. These judgments and the resulting loss of divine comfort evidence a loss of God's presence. That loss of His presence drops a congregation's divine protection. Unless they change direction, the loss of protection leads to the increase in evil. The light of the church eventually flickers out. God's patience is long but not infinite with a wayward church. Unless they demonstrate a change in their heart, the church's future may be in question. Returning to God becomes more important than ever.

On March 17th, 1680, Increase Mather preached a sermon titled, *Returning Unto God the Great Concern of a Covenant People*. Mather, an early graduate of Harvard and the first to receive a doctoral degree from that institution, served as president of Harvard on two occasions. His church, North Church in Boston, entered into a covenant with God as a result of the Solemn Assembly they held

---

[89] Ibid 79-86

in 1680.[90]   Here is an excerpt of the covenant the church embraced. Its content reveals their consciousness of their accountability before God:

> "We do also give up ourselves one unto another, in the Lord according to the will of God, freely covenanting and binding ourselves to walk together as a right ordered congregation and Church of Christ . . . And whereas the Messengers of these Churches, who have met together to enquire into the reason of the Lord's controversy with this His people, have taken notice of many provoking evils as the procuring cause of the judgments of God upon New England; so far as we, or any of us, have been guilty of sin in respect to any of them, we desire from our hearts to bewail it before the Lord and humbly to entreat for pardoning mercy for the sake of the blood of the everlasting Covenant."[91]

The covenant goes on to describe their commitments to each other in the body, their relationship with God as a body and their walk with the Lord in the home. What is clear is the association they understand between corporate sin and divine judgment/discipline on their church. This is a connection we today either fear or fail to recognize, and it is killing us.

Another Harvard graduate, William Williams, preached *The Danger of Not Reforming Known Evils*. This message, preached in Hatfield, Massachusetts in 1707, warns about ignoring sin in the histories of our churches. Williams writes:

> "The inveterateness of a disease is shown when it resists and overcomes healing medicines. Just so, when suitable means are used to bring a people to repentance and all prove frustrated and ineffectual, it shows their incorrigibility and irreclaimability . . . When there is not that humiliation, repentance, brokenness of heart for sin and humble waiting upon God for mercy that ought to be present, but when men put off God with empty shows and external devotions, they heighten rather than moderate His anger . . . It is a fact that the sins of God's professing people are the provoking causes of their calamities . . . It is the abounding of iniquities among us that has made way for the many rebukes of heaven that we have been under . . . Oh that you would consider it! Is it not better to part with the dearest lust than to be an Achan to trouble our Israel at such a time as this?"[92]

---

[90] Ibid 96.
[91] Ibid 117-118
[92] Ibid 120-141

In the years after the earthquake of 1727 and before the First Great Awakening, John Webb preached *The Duty of a Degenerate People to Pray for the Reviving of God's Work.* The occasion was a special day of fasting and prayer at the new North Church in Boston. Webb wanted to motivate believers to pray for revival. His understanding of the corporate nature of revival reflects once again the early American emphasis which we have now lost. He said:

"A thing never begins to revive until it begins to recover the life and strength and beauty it once had, nor can it be fully revived until it is fully restored to itself in these respects. Therefore, when we pray that God would revive His work among us, we pray that He would recover *us* from *our own* declensions in religion and that He would make the life and power of godliness to grow and prevail as much as ever . . . We must acknowledge that *we* do not have nearly as much of that zeal for the honor of God and of that indignation against sin as was once the glory of these *churches* . . . When we go into a *Christian assembly*, how little we have of that religious attention, love, and delight which were once to be seen in the countenances of God's people, and how few of the hearers now make it a matter of conscience to water the seed of the Word with their prayers to God. As a direct result of this neglect of means, thorough and saving conversions are comparatively rare in our *churches* . . . But alas, as though nothing of the most amazing thunders and lightnings and the most terrible earthquakes could awaken *us,* *we* are at this time fallen into as deep a sleep as ever. Indeed, there is scarcely anything of the working of God's Spirit to be seen among *us* now . . . We must pray that He will abundantly pour forth His Spirit from on high and recover these declining *churches* to their first love and their first works[93] (Italics mine).

Reading that excerpt, it's hard not to wonder "How have we become blind to the way God deals with us as *churches*?" What have we left in the dust by ignoring the corporate nature of repentance and revival? How can we expect revival to come when our churches are full of sinful attitudes and behaviors and values, and clearly under Divine discipline for it? The early preachers of this country had not yet been contaminated by the philosophy of individualism that now pervades our culture. We hear our individual walk with the Lord emphasized every Sunday. We direct people individually to go deeper with God. We speak of how God must sanctify us individually but we overlook the sanctification of our churches. What kind of bride can the Groom expect to find upon His return? All of us need to examine our hearts and more importantly we need to examine the heart of our church. The viability of our church's testimony hangs in the balance.

---

[93] Ibid 218-242

Recent examples of Solemn Assemblies

Fortunately, some churches are becoming aware of their true standing before the Living God. They have recognized God's purpose in the depths of their corporate pain. Churches, like people, often wait until they have no place to look but up before they cry out for help. But why wait until we find ourselves on Death's doorstep before we seek the Lord? Why wait until our flame is nearly extinguished before we cry out for revival?

> "He wants us to stop assuming the next great program or pastor will save our church."

It's better to go see the doctor now than to ignore your symptoms and end up in the emergency room later! The Lord longs for us to come to Him. He wants us to stop assuming the next great program or pastor will save our church. He wants us to get a clue as to the real nature of our church's problems. Until we do and until we address the real problems—the things *He* says are our problems—His blessing will be muted on every program or ministry initiative we pursue. Such was the case with the two churches I want to describe. The stories are real. Their present problems were reflections of their past problems, but once they heard what Jesus was telling them through their problems, they repented and, using a Solemn Assembly, made things right. To grasp the significance of their Solemn Assemblies, we must understand what they discovered about themselves and then what they did about it.

Church A

Their pastor had just left. On the surface he and his wife were pursuing a call to missions. Below the surface, five years of tension had percolated between the pastor and lay leaders. The church was largely made up of those who had left other churches of the same denomination for one reason or another. They found a home at "Church A," which had a park-like setting. However, the beauty outside did not extend inside. The tension boiled over when the younger half of the church left at the same time the aforementioned pastor departed for the mission field.

On a human level, there was no reason why this church should not have grown and prospered. They had a couple of lay leaders I deemed "Ten Talent Men." They were greatly gifted and had carried significant roles with other successful churches. Yet their presence in this church did not lead to ministry blessing. The pastor had worked tirelessly at building relationships with those outside the church but his hard work never translated into church growth. An Ethnic group, which met Sunday afternoon, packed out the same sanctuary that was three-quarters empty when the Anglo congregation used it on Sunday morning. Demographics did not fully explain the contrast. The city in which the church was located was growing, indeed so was the entire region. There were plenty of folks to be reached, and the church had been successful reaching them in the past, but not now, despite the pastor's best efforts.

Some might suppose the church's lack of visibility played a role in its stalled ministry. Though situated on a beautiful piece of property, the church sat near the back of it. Their signage, however, appeared adequate to let passing cars and people know they were there, and the entrance to the property appeared inviting. Regardless, the church seemed to languish.

Historical Review

In the time between the departure of their last pastor and the arrival of their next one, the lay leadership consented to review the history of their church for the purpose of discerning what Jesus was saying to them.

Much of what we discovered in this journey was positive. Through the church's thirty-year existence, they enjoyed positive ministry to youth and children, a strong Sunday School and missions programs, and for a time they were held up as a model of cutting-edge ministry. They renovated their facility just five years earlier to enhance their ministry. All these things Jesus commended. Yet their attendance figures remained erratic and, after an initial growth spurt in the early 1980s, the church never recovered its previous numerical strength.

As we examined the crises in their history, a curious pattern emerged. It seemed the relationship with every pastor they had ended badly. We discovered that their first pastor had deeply wounded the church with an adulterous affair. Their second pastor, after years of faithful ministry, got undermined by lay leaders. The next pastor departed the church so wounded that he left ministry altogether. Their last pastor had committed to be there five years and made that promise publicly. He stayed exactly five years and though his departure appeared gracious, it was not without an undercurrent of strife.

The Real Problem

What the church experienced in the present reflected what they faced repeatedly in their history. The cycles of pain reoccurred and, while they varied in their manifestations, they could not be denied. What wasn't so obvious? The underlying causes of the church's behavior. Only after several days of discussion did one person who had been at the church from the beginning share two stories that unlocked the real problem.

Eight people started the church, people who previously attended another church of the same denomination. They "said" they wanted to plant a denominational church closer to their homes. However, something odd became apparent when they started an *independent* church rather than one affiliated with their denomination. What motivated their actions?

It seems those eight were disgruntled at how a denominational leader had handled the discipline of a former pastor of the "sending church." (Ironically, that pastor's wife now *attended* this daughter church thirty years later! Her quiet presence was God's reminder of the church's real problem.) Now the issue was not how the denomination handled the discipline of that former minister, but the deception of the eight people who disguised their real intent in planting that new church. They took matters into their own hands when they chose to start what became their new church home. The church eventually became part of the denomination they left but this only occurred when they needed money to build and requested help from the denomination's development fund.

Would such a story ever have surfaced under normal operations of the church? No, but the church's beginnings did not escape the eyes of the Lord. They are too pure to overlook the evil we think we have "gotten away with." Could He bless a church that started in deception and rebellion?

The other story that confirmed this underlying problem related to the purchase of the church's lovely property. At the time the property was available, the governing board set out a fleece of sorts. If the property passed a perk test and a septic system could be installed, they would purchase the land. When the environmental engineer tested the soil, it simply would not perk. None of the locations on the property he tested met the absorption requirements for a septic system. Instead of relinquishing the right to purchase, the board had dirt hauled in to create an area that met the septic requirements. This explained why the church built at the rear of the parcel, near the septic location. The man who knew this story shared it through tears. He had known the church overstepped the Lord, not abiding by the very stipulation they set before Him. This knowledge plagued him for twenty-five years!

As the present leaders reviewed this history, they labeled the behavior founding the church, the purchase of the land, and ultimately the church's treatment of its pastors as "taking matters into their own hands." The very DNA of the church's founding carried through to the departure of their last pastor. This was the issue they felt they needed to focus on in their Solemn Assembly.

Preparation

In preparation for that Assembly, they wrote several letters of apology to previous pastors and denominational officials. They acknowledged the damage the church had done to its shepherds. All the leaders signed these letters. On the day of the Solemn Assembly, most of the lay leaders participated in the service. Some described the blessings which Christ commended, others the challenges and one shared the things Christ had against them. The man who shared the two stories with the board that helped them understand the heart of the matter now repeated those stories for the congregation. They sought to break their cycle of sin and disciplinary pain from God. They utilized mediatorial authority and identificational repentance to bring healing to the wounds caused by a previous pastor. During the open time of prayer, the congregation shared encouraging verses as well as heartfelt prayers of confession.

God's Presence was apparent during the open time of prayer. Each person in attendance placed a long-stem flower in a vase as a symbol of the restored beauty of the body of Christ. Our intent was to turn the church over to its rightful Owner, the One Who purchased it with His own blood. One key leader felt the church was finally back on the right track. Another felt it was as if the weight they had been carrying had been lifted.

It was not all sweetness. One lady abruptly left the church and wrote a scathing letter about bringing up the past. Another person, however, felt the Solemn Assembly to be one of the most meaningful services he ever experienced. People had an undeniable sense of spiritual relief. It was as if the Lord had waited for this day for decades. The rare beauty of a church repenting of their long-held sin is a joyous thing.

Church B

"Bobble-head leadership" was a new term to me. I first heard it used during the historical review of "Church B." Its meaning became clear as we looked closely at the progress of the church through the years.

I would describe it as a "neighborhood church"—one of many small churches located in neighborhoods throughout the community. They moved to their current location after fifteen years in a poorer section of town. Forty years later, the once new area they moved to had itself become older and less desirable. The town is home to a large military base. Nearly everyone works at the base or is connected to someone who does.

Initially, like most churches, they did not perceive themselves in need of corporate revival. What they felt, was their need to find a new pastor. Gradually though they came to see that underlying issues hampered their ministry, things which needed to be addressed before the next pastor arrived. Their leaders agreed to review their history.

Historical Review

We highlighted many good and commendable ministries as they began their review. Words like "dedicated" and "persevering" were used to describe the character of the church's constituency. They had a strong youth ministry since the start of the church. They enjoyed good preachers, a vibrant women's ministry and a men's breakfast that attracted men from other churches. Missions and prayer were also strengths. The church held revival meetings for years which also proved a blessing. They heard Jesus commend all these positive efforts as glorifying to His name.

But as the church had its peaks, it also had its valleys through its fifty-five year history. Four peaks and four valleys to be exact. When we charted their attendance, it resembled a jagged mountain range with a valley following each peak the church reached. The church rose to the maximum sustainable attendance given the size of its facilities, only to decline in the years following its heights. At one point it declined to the point of closure and a pioneering pastor restarted it. They suffered three drawn-out exoduses of people and one dramatic split, each leading to a "valley."

Behind the Roller Coaster Ride

What was behind this roller coaster ride? As we explored the various eras of the church Christ made it clear that the lay leadership followed whatever pastor they had, for good or for ill. Following a good pastor—and they had some—is a good thing. But lay leadership is responsible before Christ to protect the congregation from pastoral leaders who may want to lead the church astray. "Church B" had a few of these too, which caused them a load of corporate pain.

One pastor decided he wanted to be a farmer at the same time as being a pastor. He bought twenty-five acres and began to charge farm equipment to the church account! By using the church's line of credit, he was not charged tax. He thought that if he paid the bill promptly it would never get back to the church. Before long though the church got sued by the equipment company for lack of payment!

Another pastor, overly eager to see growth, authorized architectural plans to enlarge the facility. His heart was in the right place but he did not work along with the board. When he left the church, they owed $20,000 for building plans they never used.

In the early years of the church's ministry, when things were growing, a new pastoral couple came on the scene. He was a very good preacher and the previous pastor approved him as the right man for the job. However, an exodus began almost immediately. Through tears, one women shared how this pastor's wife alienated the women of the church through judgmentalism and a highly critical spirit. Over the course of four years the church's attendance was cut in half.

What would Jesus say to a church like this? It became apparent that the lay leaders had displayed great passivity in the face of pastoral misconduct. They became more concerned with moving on to the next leader than addressing the discipline that would have kept the church healthy. We settled on this passivity of the church's male lay leadership as the root cause of the church's problems. They tolerated misbehavior without discipline.

I had a hard time understanding how a church with strong ties to a military base could be so passive. If they sent personnel all over the world to step up and do difficult things, how could they be so passive in the church? When I asked that question one board member piped up, "It makes perfect sense. It's 'bobble-head leadership'." I asked him to explain, and he said, "On the base, we have no say in what we are asked to do. Our assignments get handed down to us from others with authority. We simply do what we are told." He called this "do-as-you're-told-without-questioning" approach "bobble-head leadership." We labeled it "blind submission to authority" combined with a spirit of indifference. I found it amazing that the culture on base had so completely influenced the church. In church histories we often see sin enter the camp through such localized cultural influences.

Preparation

In preparation for their Solemn Assembly, we met to deal with issues related to reconciling with a former pastor. The board also discussed getting right before God as a body. Each man had a part in the service we planned. We explained the things Christ commended through the years, the challenges He recognized the church faced and the things He had against them as a body. We shared what we believed to be the root problem and the leaders publicly signed a corporate covenant committing to break with the patterns of their past. They implemented both mediatorial authority as well as identificational repentance for the poor behavior by some of their pastors. The change in spirit actually began before the service proper. The leaders had spent time in confession before the Lord, changing the spiritual climate of the church. The most significant aspect of this change was a fresh sense of freedom and unity enjoyed among the leaders. They began to look forward to what God would do in the future.

What to Expect

Solemn Assemblies settle things before God on a corporate level. God waits for His people to take ownership of and responsibility for their painful problems which keep hindering them. Church people are prone to ignore pain and put off treatment as long as they can. So God keeps sending the painful episodes to challenge us to seek His face and hear what He is saying to us. When we go before the Lord in a Solemn Assembly, we start to function in *God's* reality. We face and address the spiritual reasons for our corporate ill health. Remember, revival brings a restoration of *spiritual health.*

> "God waits for His people to take ownership of and responsibility for their painful problems which keep hindering them."

Taking responsibility in humility before God results in a rapid improvement of the spiritual climate and the renewal of energies of your church's leadership. Hope replaces confusion and a renewed spirit replaces ministry frustration. This is the universal experience of churches honestly pursuing the Lord in this manner. Pastor Marsh Sorber of CrossPoint Church in Binghamton, New York reports, "Since the service there has been a great sense of release and joy that was missing previously. Praise The Lord! The attitude of the church has been visibly changed; you can see it on the faces of the people as we gather on Sunday mornings. There is a new sense of joy that was missing in the past."

Observers of the change in another church write, "The body of Christ was ready to look deeply to Jesus and at their history to surface what He would commend, what challenges they faced and what He might have against them in each period of the church's life. We celebrated and grieved, rejoiced and repented. Truly God's spirit was bringing cleansing, conviction, and comfort. It was a beautiful experience . . . We believe revival has begun and will spread."

One of the Elders at Barcroft Bible Church in Fairfax, Virginia reports, "We sense a growing work of God in the corporate heart of our church. Healing and hope are beginning to capture one heart at a time." Jim Bolich, pastor of Prince Street Church, reported on the change in the spirit of his church after their Solemn Assembly. He writes, "I sense clearly that the Lord of the Church, Jesus, has forgiven us. I sense a willingness among the people to extend forgiveness to one another. Now, we must learn to live as the Body of Christ."

The Lord loves His churches and longs to bless them. When a church repents, it recovers God's blessing; where their efforts seemed hampered in the past, they enjoy a new spiritual foundation on which to build their future ministry.

A Word of Caution

God takes Solemn Assemblies seriously. Once a church becomes aware of its true condition before the Lord and confesses its corporate sins, they gain both a new footing and new *accountability* for their ministry. It is one thing to live through years of a church's struggling ministry ignorant that God has a complaint against your church, but it is another thing entirely to repent of those things and then return to the same behaviors again.

I believe that, once a church repents, the Lord holds it to a new standard. He expects a change in line with the repentance. It is not unusual for a church, like an individual, to regress into its former displeasing behaviors. The question is: to what degree do they regress and have they learned from the regression? Does their regression include a recovery that shows the congregation is maturing as it grows out of its past? Or does the regression instead betray superficiality in the original repentance?

Just as an individual experiences salvation and then growth in the Lord, gradually to become sanctified from past sinful tendencies, in the same way a church becomes sanctified corporately. It is up and down, but with an overall track upward. Corporate revival represents a jump upward in spiritual life, but increasing sanctification in the pattern of its life must follow. The Lord will often test the repentance of a church by challenging its new-found liberty with difficulties. We should expect the Lord to test our corporate sincerity. He is, after all, the Lord of our church. The Groom wants to show openly what is in the heart of His Bride.

"Church A" was tested subsequent to their Solemn Assembly. They regressed so completely that, after they called their next pastor, they became embroiled in conflict within months of his arrival. The church closed its doors shortly thereafter. Their lampstand was removed from the scene.

"Church B" also faced a test after their Solemn Assembly and dealt with some regressive behavior. They recognized their lapse and brought it before the Lord. They learned through it and still have hope of being a light in their community. Picturing a church as a tree with branches (ministries) and fruit (results and growth), we can see corporate revival as "root work." It addresses the unseen network of deep spiritual roots that feed the life of the church. Corporate revival functions like fertilizer, bringing nutrients into the root system facilitating the tree to once again produce much fruit.

Often pruning needs to be done as well and God leads us to take care of it in the tests following a Solemn Assembly. Relational problems which have gone unaddressed will need to be faced. If leaders have ignored disciplining sin in the congregation, it will have to be confronted. A test will force this. If disunity or a critical spirit has caused problems, these will have to be addressed. Pruning represents an adjustment to the way the body has functioned. Once Christ makes clear what He has against our church, He expects us to rectify any of those problems on the branch level. These may have been ignored for a long time, but Christ strengthens leaders by leading them to face and deal with what they have avoided.

You must grow into a true body of believers under one roof, not just the assemblage of individuals who meet together on Sunday morning and are totally disconnected from each other. Revival is a corporate experience and benefits the overall life of the church. You want that health and vibrancy it provides to grow into a beautiful expression of Christ in your locality. It is that unique beauty Christ provides which visitors will find appealing and the lost will find attractive.

Summary

Corporate revival is exciting. Seeing a group of church leaders and a congregation make things right before the Lord is as thrilling as it gets. As we survey the Church in America, we see a nation full of local churches in dire need of corporate revival. Many are unaware of their need. Our nation's decaying culture spirals down in concert with weak churches, leaving them isolated and irrelevant as true change agents. Unless these churches gain new spiritual vibrancy, nothing will stop the secularization that suffocates Christ's bride.

What about your church? Are you willing to bet your eternal reward on the current health of your local church? If you are not so confident or if you think there could be a problem, look into your history. See what you discover. Don't let another day go by without finding out what Jesus is saying to your church. Forego the artificial church culture that may be blinding your congregation to its true state before the Lord. Dare to pray that God would restore the health of your church and your own spiritual health in the process. If we long to see this nation blessed and influence the world for Christ, we must avoid the fate suffered by the churches in Europe. They could never regain their spiritual footing. Now they are irrelevant in their cultures. We still have time, but probably not long.

Gerald Sittser writes, "Churches move slowly, just like glaciers . . . but when they do change, they can become as powerful as an advancing glacier that sweeps away everything in its path."[94] Shall we enter a new ice age that leaves us immobile, entrenched, frozen solid or can we free ourselves to become a powerful force for God in the coming decades? The choice is up to the church. Shall we seek the Lord and prepare our church's heart for revived life? The Lord Himself waits for us to do so. *"He who has an ear, let him hear what the Spirit says to the churches"* (Revelation 3:22).

---

[94] Gerald Sittser, *Water From A Deep Well.* (Downers Grove, IL: InterVarsity Press 2007) 294.

Appendix

Recurring Personal Pain

The pain we see in our local church histories is caused by the people who have made up those congregations. Thoroughly examining your church's history will reveal the part certain individual(s) played, and they may recognize how their sin and misjudgments played a role in the corporate wounding and defilement. These can be excruciatingly painful realizations for a godly leader or individual. I have seen grown men openly weep when they realized how their actions impacted the body. It is painful enough to fail the Lord in one's personal life, but when one realizes how his or her actions debilitated the body of Christ, it can be overwhelming.

Some of this pain can be avoided if we begin to understand how God uses it in our personal lives. I am not talking about the minor things like catching a cold and assuming one is under divine discipline. Rather I refer to those major episodes of pain—divorce, addiction, infidelity, a wayward child, etc.—which many endure, sometimes with little insight into God's purposes. Prudence and providence require the individual believer to explore why a major source of pain has entered his or her life.

If one's life is marked by repeated painful episodes with only brief periods of semi-sanity squeezed in between, is it beyond us to consider thoughtfully what God might be doing in our lives during such times? Now we have a biblical caution found in the account of the blind man, of whom the disciples asked Jesus, "Rabbi, who sinned, this man or his parents, that he should be born blind?" Jesus replied that neither he nor his parents sinned but "*it was in order that the works of God may be displayed in him*" (John 9:1-3). Not every pain contains a metamessage for our lives; it may instead be an opportunity to trust God in a new manner. The point is we need to ask God to show us. We must discern between times when God allows difficulty so His greater glory might be revealed and those times when He uses discipline as a corrective and shaping influence (Hebrews 4-5; 1 Corinthians 11:30-32).

When we sense God has a message in the pattern of pain we experience, we should be open to the possibility that He may be speaking to us about an unresolved issue we are carrying from our past. Once we acknowledge that possibility, it is time to seek His face for understanding and discernment to determine what it is. It takes serious courage to do this! There are reasons we have avoided doing so, just like in our churches. Some believers spend years in a personal wilderness before they learn the lesson God seeks to teach them. Until they learn it though, it hinders them from making significant progress in their lives and ministries. Just like our churches!

If we fail to hear what God says to us through our personal pain, God will mercifully cause us to face further crises because He wants us to *get over* the hindering issue. Unless we get to the root issue stopping our growth, it will hold us back from the deep experience of repentance necessary to be totally free—the objective God seeks. Wilberforce makes this observation, "Too often the things we confess are far from the things that are the true deep sins in our lives. We are each like a murderer who confesses to an occasional problem with anger."[95] God is doing this deeper work in your life and you may have never put it together. Don't be discouraged. We see biblical characters struggling with the same thing.

Joseph's Traumas

Joseph is a clear example of an individual God locked in a repeating cycle of pain until he learned what God sought to teach him. Joseph experienced three painful episodes that are recorded for us before he was able to shed all that his "coat of many colors" symbolized in his family. Joseph's varicolored tunic was a metamessage to his brothers of fatherly favoritism. It symbolized his favored status in the heart of their father Jacob.

Genesis 37 lays out Joseph's years as the teenage son of privilege. He once brought back a bad report about his brothers that inflamed their hatred of him. His dreams of being exalted over his family did not help either. Even his father thought his dreams were over the top. Nevertheless, Jacob gave him place, privilege and preeminence over his older brothers. He was, after all, the son of the wife Jacob favored most. He had been favored from the day he was born. With so much bestowed on Joseph at an early age, one imagines a subtle sense of self-importance taking root in his heart.

---

[95] Wilberforce 86.

Was Joseph a bad person? Is that why he went through so much pain? No, he was like the rest of us, a mix of traits both pleasing and displeasing to the Lord. But God knew that self-importance would hinder Joseph, so He knew it had to go before He could accomplish what He wanted to do through him. The favor and importance he enjoyed was an obstacle to God's plan for his life. It was that sense of self-importance God had to address before He could use Joseph as desired.

Trauma/Crisis #1

Through the hands of his brothers God began a humbling work in Joseph that would last twenty years. The first episode came when his brothers plotted to kill and then decided to sell Joseph off to a place where they would never see him again. Their unmasked hatred of Joseph radiates through the words of Genesis 37:19 and 20, *"And they said to one another, 'Here comes this dreamer!'" "Now then, come and let us kill him and throw him into one of the pits; and we will say, 'A wild beast devoured him.' Then let us see what will become of his dreams!"* Joseph was victimized by brothers! He was outnumbered, and helpless to resist their will. Such is the nature of the pain God may use to shape our lives. At times the odds seem entirely against us and the difficulty we face beyond our ability to cope. Joseph's confusion and pain is described by the brothers themselves years later as they remember his cries for mercy the day they sold him: *"Then they said to one another, 'Truly we are guilty concerning our brother, because we saw the distress of his soul when he pleaded with us, yet we would not listen:'"* (Genesis 42:21).

Trauma/Crisis #2

In Genesis 39 Joseph is thrown in jail by his Egyptian master because he resisted the seduction by his master's wife but could not shake her false accusation. In the face of the indecent proposal by his master's wife, Joseph said, *"Behold with me my master does not concern himself with anything in the house, and he has put all that he owns in my charge"* (vs. 8).

Does Joseph's statement reflect the desire of a faithful man longing to honor his master? There is a subtle hint of the same self-importance in his reply though. Read it again with emphasis on the words "me" and "my" and you will hear hints of Joseph's self-focus still vibrating. Verse 9 reveals Joseph's heart more clearly: *"There is no one greater in this house than I, and he has withheld nothing from me except you, because you are his wife. How could I do this great evil, and sin against God?"* Joseph longed to honor the Lord by maintaining his purity, *"How could I do this great evil, and sin against God?"* Yet from the same heart flows another statement that suggests he still wrestles with his place of privilege and standing, *"There is no one greater in this house than I."* Why does he feel the need to exclaim that?

There was someone with greater influence in the house than himself and her name was Mrs. Potiphar! Then, with typical biblical symbolic pattern—the way God still does it in our lives and in our churches so we don't miss His point—there is the "cloak" she stripped off of him and used as false evidence. Wherever Joseph went, people stripped cloaks—that first symbol of his self-importance—off of him and used them as evidence. God sought to do a work in Joseph's heart in relation to his sense of privilege. The crises were different but in both cases God pointed clearly to the same underlying issue in Joseph's life.

Trauma/Crisis #3

The third crisis comes in Genesis 40. Joseph's leadership skills resulted in his ultimately managing the jail where the false charges landed him. Later they assigned two royal officials to Joseph's charge. One night they both had dreams and, in the morning, both men felt disturbed over the significance of them. Joseph offered to interpret each dream and again, in his interaction with the two men, we get a glimpse into his heart. He said to the chief cupbearer, *"Do not interpretations belong to God? Tell it to me, please"* (vs. 8). Is there an undertone of arrogance in this exchange? Probably not, for Joseph demonstrates a willingness to give glory to God for the ability to interpret dreams. It appears the path of humility God has placed him on worked. He does not betray the self-importance the earlier episodes suggest. However, after Joseph gives the interpretations, he blurts out in frustration, *"Please do me a kindness by mentioning me to Pharaoh and get me out of this house . . . for I have done nothing that they should have put me into the dungeon"* (vs. 14-15).

Hmmm. How is it Joseph sees God's hand in his ability to interpret dreams, but does not recognize God's hand in placing him in the prison? Most of us have a hard time believing that we deserve the pain we encounter, let alone that God might be behind it as He attempts to get us to face things so we can heal. We see them as the result of injustice at the hands of others, *"For I was in fact kidnapped from the land of the Hebrews."* In times like these we desperately want to escape the limitations God may place on us to get us to face things. Joseph said, *"do me a kindness by mentioning me to Pharaoh."* He sought ways to get out of jail and he imagined Pharaoh's official might use his influence to help him. We feel his frustration, his desperation and his anger when he says, *"get me out of this house,*" but do we hear his humility or faith? Doesn't he instead sound obsessed with escaping his humiliating circumstances? Who does not want to escape a bad upbringing, a bad marriage, or a bad job? But perhaps God is doing more in us through these experiences than we realize.

Joseph finishes his statement with, "*for I have done nothing that they should have put me into the dungeon.*" Legally speaking, Joseph is absolutely right. He faced a terrible injustice against which he felt powerless. How can God be in that? And yet God was in it. It was part of God's plan for Joseph to put him where he could face and learn those painful lessons necessary to free him from what his upbringing did to him. Then God wanted him to advance His plan for His people.

Simultaneously, God refined Joseph through these circumstances. God needed a yielded, humble and pliable Joseph for His plan to work. Joseph needed to trust God in the midst of his difficulties but not simply to get out of them. He patiently waited for Joseph to come to the end of himself. He puts us through our challenges waiting for the same.

Joseph failed to see that his brothers, Mrs. Potiphar and the forgetful cupbearer were God's tools to break his pride and self-importance. God decides to keep Joseph under lock and key for a while longer. We read, "*Yet the chief cupbearer did not remember Joseph, but forgot him*" (vs. 23). Is there anything more humiliating to the self-important individual than to be forgotten? Pharaoh's official totally forgets him. He languishes in jail for another "two full years" (Genesis 41:1).

Joseph Gets It

But something happens to Joseph in the next twenty-four months. By the time he stands before Pharaoh, he is a changed man. Somewhere in those two additional years in prison Joseph came to the end of himself. He yields to God's sovereignty and relinquishes his self-importance. When Pharaoh said to Joseph in Genesis 41:15, "*I have heard it said about you, that when you hear a dream you can interpret it.*" Joseph replies with complete transparency, "*It is not in me; God will give Pharaoh a favorable answer.*" Even more obvious is what he does not say; he does not ask Pharaoh for a pardon, nor does he belabor his innocence or barter a release for the interpretation of the dream. Gone is the self-importance that marked his prior life.

Somewhere in those last years of imprisonment Joseph yielded his heart to God in a way he had not done previously. As a result we see, for the first time in a long time, someone puts clothing on Joseph rather than stripping it off, and this time it's permanent. Genesis 41:42 recounts what happened: *"Then Pharaoh took off his signet ring from his hand, and put it on Joseph's hand, and clothed him in garments of fine linen and put a gold necklace around his neck."*

The clothing Pharaoh placed on Joseph represented the same kind of favor and elevation as the "coat of many colors" Joseph received from his father. The clothing of Joseph's life symbolizes where he is in his spiritual journey, his place, position, prestige and importance. When Pharaoh outfits Joseph, the meaning of the clothing completes and affirms his arrival to the fullness of God's purpose. So what has changed? Joseph has changed! He learned through the painful episodes in his life to release his self-importance and pride, and humbly to receive whatever God had for him. That's the only way God or Pharaoh could trust him with the level of responsibility he received. It is also the only way Joseph could say to his brothers in Genesis 50:20, *"And as for you, you meant evil against me, but God meant it for good."* He finally learned from the pattern of painful discipline rather than fighting or ignoring it.

What is God saying to you through the many difficulties you have faced? Is there an underlying pattern to the pain you have failed to recognize? He is not being mean or cruel. He wants to sanctify, heal and prepare us, but will not allow us to circumvent a root issue, any more than He allows our church to do so.

Why continue to go through repeated difficulties? They can end if you face them and ask God to give you insight into the pain He has allowed in your life. Try to get a historical perspective on your life. Seek His face and ask Him, "What is really going on here?" It's time to get off the treadmill of divine discipline as Joseph finally did and begin a new era of blessing in your life - as you yield more thoroughly to God.

Revival, personal and corporate, awaits.

Bibliography

Augustine. *The City of God*. New York: Random House, Marcus Dods DD Translator, 1993.

Bartleman, Frank. Azusa Street. New Kensington, PA:Whitaker House, 1982.

Bauer, Walter. *A Greek-English Lexicon of The New Testament*. Chicago IL: The University of Chicago Press, 1979.

Bromiley, Geoffrey W. Theological *Dictionary of the New Testament Abridged in One Volume*. Grand Rapids MI: Eerdmans Publishing House, 1985

Cymbala, Jim. *Fresh Wind, Fresh Fire*. Grand Rapids MI: Zondervan Publishing House, 1997.

Dawson, John. *Healing America's Wounds*. Ventura, CA: Regal Books, 1994.

Duin, Julia. Christian World View – an Interview with Ravi Zacharias. The Washington Times: New World Communications, Inc. 2003

Ebel, John E. Thoughts Concerning Earthquake Sources in the Northeastern U.S. Presented to the USGS CEUS Workshop May 9, 2006, <usgs.gov/ research/hazmaps/whats_new/workshops/CEUSWORKSHP/Tuesday/ EbelNatSeismHazWkshpTalk.pdf>

Finney, Charles G. *Revivals of Religion*. Virginia Beach VA: CBN University Press, 1978.

Fitchett, W.H. *Wesley and His Century*. New York: Eaton and Mains, 1906.

Fogel, Robert William, *The Fourth Great Awakening and Future of Egalitarianism*. Chicago, IL, University of Chicago Press, 2000.

Havner, Vance. *Messages on Revival*. Grand Rapids MI: Baker Book House, 1958.

Havner, Vance. *On This Rock I Stand*. Grand Rapids MI: Baker Book House, 1981.

Jurgens, William A. *The Faith of the Early Fathers Vol. 3*. Collegeville, MN: The Liturgical Press, 1979.

King James Version of the Bible.

King, Martin Luther. *Letters from a Birmingham Jail*. http://www.stanford.edu/group/king/popular_requests/frequentdocs/birmingham.pdf

Lloyd – Jones, Martin. *Revival*. Westchester IL: Crossway Books, 1987

McFadden, Dorothy L., Van Dyke, Mildred D., & Johnston, Eileen L. *The Presbyterian Church* Basking Ridge NJ A History. www.brpc.org/publicationsBRPCHistory1717-1989.pdf.

Murray, Andrew. *Humility*. Kensington, PA: Whitaker House, 1982.

Murray, Andrew. *The Ministry of Intercession*. New Kensington PA: Whitaker House, 1982.

New American Standard Bible. The Lockman Foundation, 1977.

New International Version of the Bible. Nashville, TN: Broadman and Holman Publishers, 1986.

Olford, Stephen. *Lord, Open the Heavens!* Wheaton IL: Harold Shaw Publishers, 1980.

Olson, David T. *The American Church in Crisis*. Grand Rapid, MI; Zondervan, 2008.

Orr, J Edwin. *The Second Evangelical Awakening*. London: Marshall, Morgan and Scott, 1949.

Peck, Scott M. *A World Waiting to be Born*. New York: Bantam Books, 1993.

Peck, Scott M. *People of the Lie*. New York: Touchstone Books, 1983.

Perley, Sindney, The Earthquake of 1727, USGS 17 Sept. 2008
<http://earthquake.usgs.gov/regional/states/events/1727_11_10_hs.php>

Porteur and Stinton. *The Works of Thomas Secker. Vo. V*. Quoted by A. Skivington Wood. *The Inextinguishable Blaze: Spiritual Renewal and Advance in the Eighteenth Century*. Grand Rapids MI: Eerdmans Publishing Company, 1960

Quick, Kenneth, *Church and Community Exegesis*. Washington DC: Capital Bible Seminary Class Notes, 2006.

Quick, Kenneth. *Healing the Heart of Your Church*. Church Smart, 2003.

Ravenhill, Leonard. *America is too Young to Die*. Minneapolis, MN: Bethany Fellowship Inc, 1979.

Roberts, Richard Owen. *Repentance*. Wheaton, IL: Crossway Books, 2002.

Roberts, Richard Owen. *Sanctify the Congregation*. Wheaton, IL: International Awakening Press, 1994.

Schaeffer, Francis A. *The Great Evangelical Disaster*. Westchester, Il : Crossway Books, 1984.

Shaw, S.B. *The Great Revival in Wales*. Pensacola, FL: Christian Life Books, 2002.

Shaw, S. B. *Touching Incidents and Remarkable Answers to Prayer*. Chicago IL: Shaw Publishers, 1897.

Simonson, Harold P. *Selected Writings of Jonathan Edwards*. New York, Frederick Ungar Publishing Co,1970.

Stott, John. *The Living Church*. Downers Grove, IL: IVP Books, 2007.

Strong, James. *A Concise Dictionary of the Words in the Hebrew Bible*. Nashville, TN: Thomas Nelson, 1984.

Synan, Vinson. *The Holiness – Pentecostal Tradition*, Grand Rapids, IL: Eerdmans, 1997.

Tannen, Deborah. *You Just Don't Understand: Men and Women in Conversation.* Quill, 2001

Tozer, A.W. *Born After Midnight.* Harrisburg, PA: Christian Publications, 1959.
Tozer, A.W. *Paths to Power.* Harrisburg, PA: Christian Publications.

Weakley, Clair George Jr. *The Nature of Revival.* Minneapolis MN: Bethany House Publishers, 1987.

Wall, Mark A. The Puzzling Faith of Abraham Lincoln. *Christian History Magazine*, Issue 33 Vol. XI, No. 1.

Walvord, John F. & Zuck, Roy B. *The Bible Knowledge Commentary Old Testament, Haggai.* Wheaton, IL: SP Publications, 1985.

White, John. *When the Spirit Comes with Power.* Downers Grove, IL: Intervarsity Press, 1988.

Wilberforce, William. *Real Christianity.* Ventura, CA: Regal Books, 2006.